Making Two Halves a Whole

Studies for Parents in Blended Families

Lonni Collins Pratt

David C. Cook Publishing Co., Elgin, Illinois—Paris, Ontario

Scripture quotations, unless otherwise noted, are from the *Holy Bible, New International Version* (NIV). © 1973, 1978, 1984 by International Bible Society. Used by permission of Zondervan Publishing House.

850 N. Grove Ave., Elgin, IL 60120-2892
Cable address: DCCOOK
Cover designers: Tom Schild and Jack Foster
Cover illustrator: Pete Whyte
Illustrator: Guy Wolek
Product Developer: Terri Hibbard
Editors: Dave and Neta Jackson
Printed in U.S.A.

ISBN: 0-7814-5138-8

1   2   3   4   5   6   7   8   9   10

Contents

Welcome to Family Growth Electives

Congratulations! The fact that you are using a study in the Family Growth Electives series says that you are concerned about today's families. You and your group of adults are about to begin an exciting adventure.

Each course in this series has been created with today's families in mind. Rather than taking a single topic and applying it to all adults, these Family Growth Electives treat each adult life stage or situation separately. This means that people who are approaching or going through similar stages or situations in life can get together to share and study their common needs from a biblical perspective.

The concept of family life stages comes from the work of Dr. Dennis B. Guernsey, associate professor of Marital and Family Therapy, Fuller Theological Seminary. Guernsey says that the family has critical tasks to accomplish at each stage in order to nurture healthy Christians.

Many adults in churches today have not come from strong Christian roots. Others may have attended church as children, drifted away during their adolescent or young adult years, and are now back in church in an effort to get help with the everyday problems of family life.

Most adults do not have the benefits of living near their extended family. The church can meet the needs of such people by becoming their "family." It can also help strengthen families by teaching them biblical principles and giving opportunities for applying those principles. That's exactly what you'll be doing as you lead your group in this Family Growth Electives study.

Dave and Neta Jackson, Editors

Introduction

This course is for parents in blended families.

Forging a healthy, happy blended family is a big challenge. According to recent U.S. census figures, about 70 percent of stepfamilies dissolve within ten years. The purpose of this course is to equip the parents to effectively navigate their turbulent times and celebrate the growth and joy of a "second chance."

Whenever a family divides and another group of individuals attempts to blend as a new family, there are disappointments. Some family members wish it could have been different. Some remember painful, possibly even abusive incidents.

The couple themselves must deal with the memories and fears left over from another marriage. If they were rejected, they may fear it will happen again. Or they may doubt their ability to love, trust, or be faithful.

And then there is the task of loving someone else's children.

Your group members will gain a biblical perspective and learn many helpful tips about all these areas of family life as they participate in the active learning in this course. You'll find activities for group members to do alone, as couples, in small groups, and with the entire group together.

As the leader, you will find this course easy to prepare and easy to use. Each forty-five- to sixty-minute session includes step-by-step instructions printed in regular type. Each session begins with "Getting Ready" which lists everything you need to do before group time. To help pace yourself according to your available time, there are suggested time frames for each step.

All content is Scripture based. At the beginning of each session plan you will find a list of the Scriptures to be covered.

Things you might say aloud to your group are in **bold type**. Of course, it is always best to restate things in your own words. Suggested answers to questions are in parentheses.

Each of the thirteen sessions has reproducible resource sheets. In most cases you will use these as handouts for group members. It would also work to turn some of the resources into overhead transparencies if you'd like.

Making Two Halves a Whole can be a source of encouragement and growth for your group members—growth in their relationship with the Lord, each other, and their children.

Dangerous Expectations

1

Session Aim:
To help couples establish realistic expectations of remarriage and self and their relationships with each other and their children.

Weddings are about bright futures and dreams coming true. This is so whether the couple is twenty or eighty years old.

When all the celebration has calmed down and a remarried couple gets down to the business of living happily ever after, they are likely to collide with obstacles.

Stepfamilies are families born of loss. There's no getting around it. They face unique challenges and often find themselves in the middle of failure again. About 60 percent of all second marriages dissolve in divorce.[1]

That's a discouraging statistic, but it isn't a law of the universe like gravity. Stepfamilies can survive and even thrive. However, it won't happen automatically. It will take a lot of work, love, and prayer. Any remarried couple not recognizing this fact harbors a boat-load of false and dangerous expectations.

In this session, your group will delve into their expectations of remarriage. It will help couples face the challenges of a stepfamily realistically and yet with hope. It will also help them understand that God is FOR them.

As community is built in the group, encourage the members to discuss the unique problems they face and pray for one another. That process is initiated in this session, but it will need careful nurturing from the leader.

All stepfamilies are complicated . . . and each is special.

Getting Ready

Scriptures:
Matthew 19:5, 6; Ephesians 5:21; I Corinthians 7:3,4; 13:4-7; Song of Songs 2:10-13, 16, 17; Genesis 2:24; Psalms 28:7, 8; 29:11; 32:7; 33:4, 5, 18, 22; 62:1-8; 94:19; 103:2-6.

1. Prepare enough copies of the "A Portrait of Our Family" (RS-1A), "Great Expectations" (RS-1B), and "Expectation Adjustments" (RS-1C) for everyone. One per couple of RS-1A is sufficient, but every group member should have a copy of the others.
2. Prepare the area where the group will meet. Be sure of proper lighting, comfortable seating, and supplies—newsprint or a board to write on, pens, pencils, markers, sheets of blank notebook paper, Bibles, tape or tacks for hanging family portraits, and name tags.
3. Using RS-1A, prepare a family portrait of your own family or be prepared to talk about how your life has been influenced by blended families. Your willingness to model open sharing will set the tone in the group.
4. Check with your church or local library about the availability of books on the reading list (at the end of the sessions). Make copies of this list for participants to take as they wish.
5. If you plan to have group members keep individual notebooks of their resource sheets, personal notes, etc., be sure to use a three-hole punch on the resource sheets. Have three ring notebooks for purchase if this is part of your plan, or remind participants to bring one.

❶ What Do Stepfamilies Look Like?

Objective:
To help group members recognize that all families have similarities and differences and that stepfamilies are unique (10 minutes).

Welcome the couples, and encourage everyone to wear a name tag with their wedding date on it. Pass out a copy of "A Family Portrait" (RS-1A) to each couple, and ask them to fill it out.

Introduce yourself as the couples are working on the resource sheet. After a few minutes, get out the RS-1A resource sheet of your own family you prepared ahead of time and share its information with them. Be sure to be brief and to the point to set the pace for the rest of the group. Then ask each couple to do the same.

The group members will get to know one another, and they will also see that all stepfamilies are complicated—it isn't just them and their children. Stepfamilies come in all ages and situations. Some have children visiting, some don't. Some have young children, some don't. Some have their own children. Emphasize that like all families, stepfamilies are different from one another and each is very special.

Be sensitive to any nonbelievers in the group. Don't assume that they can easily find references in the Bible.

Keep to the allowed time limit by encouraging everyone to keep their introduction short and simple. Some people might not be comfortable sharing personal information and will stop talking after a simple family description. This is nothing to be concerned about. It often takes time for a small group to build trust and open up. You can encourage the process of community by sharing as honestly as you can and giving the parents opportunities to get to know one another.

Be sensitive if there are any nonbelievers in the group. Explain that you frequently refer to the Bible because as a Christian you consider it God's manual for how best to solve life's problems. Don't assume that they can easily find references in the Bible.

❷ Naming the Expectations

Objective:
To help couples develop a clearer picture of their expectations (10 minutes).

Write the following on the board or a sheet of newsprint:

A. I agree completely.
B. I agree somewhat.
C. I disagree somewhat.
D. I don't agree at all.

Give everyone a blank sheet of paper and ask group members to number one through fifteen down the left hand side of their sheets. Explain that you are going to read some typical expectations of remarried couples. They should quickly respond to each by writing the letter of their response opposite the appropriate number.

Tell the group members that you will hand out a copy of the expectations later so they can study how they responded to each. Explain that this information is for their private use and will not be shared with the group.

Read the expectation list from "Great Expectations" (RS-1B) being sure to state the number of each expectation. Do not pass out copies of RS-1B until you have gone through the complete list of expectations giving only a few seconds for group members to respond to each. This will help their responses be more spontaneous and honest.

When you have finished, distribute copies of RS-1B and have the couples transfer their quick responses to the sheet. This may be an emotional exercise for some, and the people might just want to take a deep breath and think about it a little.

Stepfamilies are formed primarily in two ways— divorce and death. This means they are born out of loss.

❸ Marriage Realities in the Bible

Objective:
To help couples understand biblical expectations of human relationships, including marriage and family (15 minutes).

By the year 2000, according to the U.S. Census Bureau, stepfamilies will be the predominant family type in America.

To some degree, stepfamilies have received bad press, especially stepmothers. Some people assume that in a stepfamily there is manipulation, resentment, injustice, and bitterness. And honestly, sometimes these things happen, but not always, and it doesn't have to be so.

Stepfamilies are formed primarily in two ways— divorce and death.

This means that stepfamilies are families born of loss. We can't escape this reality. Stepfamilies are not like first-marriage families. Everyone enters the fledgling new family with disappointments and expectations, and these are most often based on the first marriage even when we are unaware of it.

We need a guide by which to measure the appropriateness of our expectations, and Scripture provides that guide.

As volunteers read aloud the following passages of Scripture, ask the group members to identify the marriage and family expectations that are stated or implied in each passage. Remind the group that expectations in personal relationships can be frustrating when unmet. List the participants' responses on the board or newsprint. If the points in parentheses are not mentioned, add them to the list.

Matthew 19:5, 6—(unity, commitment for a lifetime)
Ephesians 5:21—(mutual submission)
I Corinthians 13:4-7—(love, patience, kindness, truthfulness, protection, trust, respect)
I Corinthians 7:3, 4—(physical intimacy)
Song of Songs 2:10-13, 16, 17—(romance, physical intimacy, faithfulness)
Genesis 2:24—(companionship, fidelity)

As a good Bible study habit, be careful not to list anything that is not specifically mentioned in the verses, even though it might have a scriptural basis in some other passage.

Linda Raney Wright, a Christian author writing on the marriage relationship, says, "In Genesis 1 and 2 we see that God developed Adam and Eve as a mutual

union, not an organization, a political hierarchy, or a parent-child relationship. God gave both man and woman the same likeness, the same blessing, responsibility, authority, provision, partnership; and then He made them 'one flesh'—a union." [2]

Briefly discuss the group's expectations of what it means to be "one flesh." Stress these points: It doesn't mean you always agree, and it doesn't mean you rely on only your spouse for your emotional fulfillment. Sometime in the discussion it should be understood that "one flesh" refers to a mystical union of intimacy and complete acceptance.

Ask the group to silently review their expectations from RS-1B and make any notes about new insights or thoughts gleaned from this study.

❹ Facing Ourselves and Our Expectations

Objective:
To encourage individuals to write realistic, biblical expectations for their own marriages and stepfamilies (10-25 minutes).

Expectations, like a secret cancer, tend to grow while we aren't paying attention. When expectations aren't discussed and admitted, they get out of hand and become unreasonable.

Often, when I expect too much from those around me, I am not leaning hard enough on God for my happiness, I am expecting too little from God.

A relationship with God is intended to provide human beings with certain foundational qualities. These are things we can receive only from and in relationship with Him.

Divide the group into two sections. Give each group a set of passages:

Group One: Psalms 28:7, 8; 29:11; 32:7; 33:4, 5, 18, 22.
Group Two: Psalms 62:1-8; 94:19; 103:2-6.

Instruct each group to make a list of what these passages state about specific things we receive in relationship with God.

Bring the group back together, and ask them to share their findings. Their responses should include the following ideas:

Group One
1. *Psalm 28:7, 8*—(strength, help, joy, salvation)
2. *Psalm 29:11*—(strength, peace)
3. *Psalm 32:7*—(protection, hiding place, songs of deliverance; refers to hope and optimism)

When we expect others to fill the God-shaped place in our souls, we are doomed to disappointment.

4. *Psalm 33:4, 5, 18, 22*—(truth, faithfulness, justice, unfailing love, watchfulness, unfailing love, and more unfailing love)

Group Two

1. *Psalm 62:1, 2, 5-8*—(only place of rest, salvation, protection, security, hope, honor, refuge, trustworthiness, someone to talk to)
2. *Psalm 94:19*—(joy and release from anxiety)
3. *Psalm 103:2-6*—(forgiveness, healing, rescue, reward, compassion, satisfaction for desires, endurance)

Taken together, what do these passages tell us about human needs and how these are met? (Responses should include: Only God can meet the fullness of human expectations and needs. If we depend on anyone but God for our deepest needs, we will be disappointed. Only God's love never fails.)

Marriages end and people are often hurt, not so much by the offenses of others, but simply because of expecting too much or the wrong things. We are all imperfect, fallen people. When we expect others to fill the God-shaped place in our souls, we are doomed to disappointment.

If time allows, do the following roleplay to discover how our loved ones might react to demanding expectations. (If you are short on time, move on to passing out "Expectation Adjustments" RS-1C). Ask for two volunteer men and two volunteer women and have the women sit side by side as a team and the men do the same.

Alternate between teams. Within each team, have the team members take turns in rephrasing expectations from their resource list on RS-1B, personalizing the expectation by making up the statement as if they were talking to a friend. The expectations need not be ones with which they agree. This is just a roleplay.

After each expectation is stated, let the teammate honestly respond with a little friendly counsel. For example:

Woman One: I've had to raise these children alone for a long time, and I think it's reasonable to expect my new husband to take the load off me now.

Woman Two: Wait a moment. I thought you married this guy because you loved him. It almost sounds like you were looking for a babysitter. Isn't that a little selfish and unreasonable?

Pray for God's blessing and increased understanding for the parents, stepfamilies, and couples.

Man One: You know, my ex-wife was never a very loving person. But with my new wife, I know my children will see what love really means because she will love them as they have never been loved.

Man Two: Hey, man, I'm glad your new wife seems more loving, but you know, only God can give your kids the kind of love they really need. If you put that expectation on your wife . . . well, I mean, how's she gonna fulfill it?

Alternate between the teams—women, men, women, men—until everyone has had a chance to express two expectations and respond twice.

Ask the group to look over their own copies of "Great Expectations" (RS-1B) again and make any more notes on their earlier responses while you pass out "Expectation Adjustments" (RS-1C).

This work sheet lists five attitudes that can change what you expect from others. Read these over, then fill out the work sheet.

Allow everyone to quietly complete this task, but reserve time to suggest that couples review together what they wrote on the bottom of the work sheet. Encourage each couple to write a joint expectation for their stepfamily according to what they understand God wants for marriage and family.

Close the session by asking for prayer concerns from the families represented in the group. Have each couple pair up with another couple for prayer during the week. Have the couples exchange names and phone numbers and, if they are willing, their family portraits as a reminder.

When you close in prayer, pray for God's blessing and increased understanding as this group moves into discovering more about themselves as stepfamilies and couples.

Notes:

1. Barbara Kantrowitz and Pat Wingert, "Step by Step: Who Will We Be?," *Newsweek*, Special Issue Winter/Spring, 1990, Volume 114, 27.

2. Linda Raney Wright, *A Cord of Three Strands* (Old Tappan, N.J.: Fleming H. Revell, 1987), 51.

Priority One: Your Marriage

2

Session Aim:
To help the remarried couple find practical ways of putting their marriage first and developing oneness with each other.

Listen: marriage begins when two people make the clear, unqualified promise to be faithful, each to the other, until the end of their days . . . a promise made, a promise witnessed, a promise heard, remembered, and trusted—this is the groundwork of marriage. Not emotions.

No, not even love. . . . Here is a marvelous work, performed by those who are made in the image of God—for we create, in this promise, a new thing, a changeless stability in an ever-changing world. . . . We have called forth a spiritual house in which each of us may dwell securely. Whether we know it or not, it is a divine thing we do, and it is holy.

—Walter Wangerin[1]

The strength of the stepfamily rests on two foundational pillars: first, the strength of each mate's faith in God and his or her willingness to put God always and consciously first, before anyone or anything else; second, the strength of the marriage. This will grow in time if both spouses purposely make their marriage top priority, second only to God.

This session will address both issues because these are interdependent. Unless a person puts God first, he or she has very little to give in marriage and will rarely put a high enough value on the married relationship.

Ask what the compiled datebook page says about how much group members value God and one another.

Getting Ready

Scriptures:
Genesis 1:27; 2:18, 23; 2:24, 25.

1. Each Scripture selection should be printed in black marker on a separate unlined index card. For this study, use the New Revised Standard Version if possible, which uses inclusive language for "man," etc.
2. Make photocopies of "Who Really Matters?" (RS-2A), "Pictures of a Marriage" (RS-2B), "Intimacy Busters" (RS-2C), and "Actions Speak Louder Than Words" (RS-2D). Every person will need their own copies. Remember to use a three-hole punch if the group members are keeping individual notebooks.
3. Ahead of time, prepare a large version of the datebook from RS-2A on white poster board or large newsprint. Across the top write: "Sunday: The Day of Most Choice." Leave enough space to write inside of each time division. Also, have available a second poster board or sheet of newsprint if you will be using the datebook again for the last step.
4. Provide colored pencils, crayons, or colored markers to use with RS-2B.

❶ Spend Some Time

Objective:
To help group members determine where and how they are spending time and what their habits say about their priorities (10 minutes).

Get out the large datebook page you prepared in advance on newsprint or poster board. Ask someone to distribute "Who Really Matters?" (RS-2A).

Ask each person to fill out their datebook according to a typical Sunday explaining that Sunday is probably the day in the week when many people have the most discretionary time. Read the following from the top of your poster before they start: **Sunday: The Day of Most Choice**.

Give the parents a few minutes to complete the activity, then ask the group members to share some of the things that they wrote by their time periods starting with the morning. Write these in the spaces on the poster datebook. Try to have two or three entries for most time periods.

If devotions, prayer, talking to each other, romance or physical intimacy, or meals together are not mentioned, ask group members when these fit and and to add them. If you have any nonbelievers in the group, include explanations of why devotions and prayer are important.

When completed, ask what the compiled datebook page says about how much group members value God and one another. Remind them that Sunday may represent an ideal day, rather than a routine weekday. Compare the actual time people spend together or alone with God to other activities. In guiding the discussion, make these points:

1. What we do with our time tells us and others what we consider most important.

2. Apart from necessities and regularly scheduled activities, most of us are consumed with whatever needs doing at the moment and seldom think beyond that.

3. We often do not spend adequate amounts of time with God or together as a couple.

4. Time does say something about what we consider important.

5. Changing our patterns requires choice and effort.

❷ God's Design for Intimacy

Objective:
To help the couples understand the design of God in their marriages (15-20 minutes).

Share this introduction with the group: **Walter Wangerin, the author of** *As for Me and My House,* **explains that God's design for marriage centers on intimate union. In our marriages we reflect and witness to the love of the Godhead and the love of Christ for His church. He writes that Adam and Eve were given to one another in the first human community. Part of our being fully human happens only in community and this is part of the created design, before the human race fell into sin.**

Give volunteers the cards printed with Genesis 1:27; 2:18, 23; and 2:24, 25 to read. Should anyone ask, you can explain that the verses are from the New Revised Standard Version which clarifies the vagueness of the terms "Adam," "man," and "human."

As they read, list these terms on the board:

Image of God
Helper
Bone of my bones
Clings

Ask the group members to share what these terms mean to them. Be sure these points are clearly established during the discussion:

"Image of God"—(The image of God is completed in the creation of male and female. Without both, it isn't whole. A couple shares the image of God because God's love requires relationship. God's love is poured out and given to another.

This love is reflected in marriage. The image of God is found in community and not merely individuals. Love must have a focus, an object, someone to give itself to.)

"Helper"—(The word "helper" does not mean inferior or less capable; it also does not mean apprentice or assistant. The same Hebrew word translated "helper" is used to refer to God in the Psalms when David calls God his Helper. [See, for instance, Ps. 121:1, 2.] This Hebrew word is used twenty-one times in the Old Testament; fourteen of those refer to God. It means one who enables, sustains, strengthens, or "comes along beside.")

"Bone of my bones"—(Made of the same substance, reflections of one another. It does not imply possession or ownership. It does not mean "mine" but "like me.")

"Clings"—(Unites, adheres, joined with.)

Point out that each of these phrases are word pictures explaining and underscoring God's design for marriage intimacy. Say something like: **How many of you would agree that when a couple is actually loving as intimately as these images portray, they will make their marriage top priority?** Guide a very brief discussion to the conclusion that when a relationship is honestly intimate, the couple will value it highly and act accordingly.

Pass out "Pictures of a Marriage" (RS-2B) and colored pencils or markers, and ask everyone to draw pictures for each word phrase. Remind them not to use any words at all. If you have an hour session, encourage the group members to pass their completed works of art around the room when finished.

❸ Intimacy Obstacles in Remarriage

Objective:
To help participants understand intimacy obstacles to making their marriages a top priority (10-15 minutes).

Of course, many things can get in the way of marital intimacy. But some are especially likely to occur in remarriage. According to the United Methodist News Service,[2] there are three obstacles to intimacy faced in remarriage: early marriage idealization, adjustment of stepchildren, and heightened fear of intimacy caused by past pain.

What are your ideas about why these three are particular problems?

Keep this discussion short and focused. Draw out three important responses, writing them on the board for emphasis:

Fear of intimacy may cause us to avoid intimacy.

(1. Idealization prevents honest sharing of yourself and acceptance of another human being.

2. Children create a situation foreign to other newlyweds and a potential problem.

3. Fear of intimacy may cause us to avoid intimacy.)

Divide the group in half, preferably by gender. Then distribute "Intimacy Busters" (RS-2C). Read the instructions out loud and give the group members a chance to ask questions before they begin the activity. Try to keep the activity light and fun. Be careful you don't allow too much time for this part of the session. Encourage the participants to work quickly.

After a few minutes, allow each group to present their information. You may find you have a few comedians in the group, and that's great. If you have a full hour for your session, encourage a general discussion of the behaviors.

End this part of the session by writing on the board: **Have I used any of these behaviors in my marriage?**

Then say: **The easy part of any discussion is talking about hypothetical situations. For just a minute, let's consider our marriages. In the last month, can you think of a time when you've fallen into the trap of intimacy busting? Let's take a minute now to prayerfully consider that question.**

As you lead in prayer, ask the Holy Spirit to reveal any instances of intimacy busting as you wait in a moment of silence. After about one minute, break the silence by suggesting that the group members use the back of the resource sheets to write down anything that came to their minds.

If anyone demonstrates willingness to talk about an instance of intimacy busting, allow that to happen, but try to keep the sharing short. Sometimes this kind of open sharing feels like pressure to talk for the more inhibited members of the group. Be sure that everyone understands there is no pressure to share the personal details of their marriages.

If your group has no more time, pass out "Actions Speak Louder Than Words" (RS-2D) and suggest that the couples use some of the ideas during the week, then close in prayer.

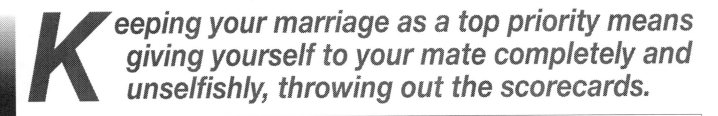

Keeping your marriage as a top priority means giving yourself to your mate completely and unselfishly, throwing out the scorecards.

❹ Decide to Act

Objective:
To encourage the couples to commit themselves to spending special time together and making their marriages top priority (10-15 minutes).

If time allows doing this step during the group time, reconvene the group so that couples are together and say: **Keeping your marriage as a top priority means giving yourself to your mate completely and unselfishly, throwing out the scorecards for who did the nicest thing last or worrying about what is owed to you.**

Refer to "Actions Speak Louder Than Words" (RS-2D), and suggest that each couple take a few minutes to look over the list of possible actions and put stars next to those that might work for them. Give them about five minutes before asking the group to share their ideas.

After a few minutes, again display the compiled datebook poster. On a second poster board or sheet of newsprint, print the last name of each couple. Ask the couples to commit themselves to take one suggested action this week. Record each commitment beside the appropriate last name.

Before closing in prayer remind the group members: **The surest way of making and keeping your marriage a top priority is by making God your top priority. Some people think that love is like apples, the more you give away, the less you have. But, when we love God with our whole selves we are enabled to love others more deeply, completely, and faithfully than we otherwise could.**

This is a good place to emphasize that many Christian marriage and family experts suggest regular periods of prayer and devotions for a couple. Be sure this doesn't sound like a "have-to."

Close the session by praying that God will help each person keep his or her priorities in order and bless the couples' efforts to grow into the intimate unions He intends. If some members of the group have shared themselves on a new level, acknowledge this by thanking God for the trust developing in the group.

Notes:

1. Walter Wangerin, Jr., *As for Me and My House* (Nashville: Thomas Nelson Publishers, 1990), p. 18.
2. Garlinda Burton, "Step-families," United Methodist News Service, August 2, 1990, p. 1.

Unpacking Old Baggage

3

Session Aim:
To help blended families cope with the pain and fears carried into the new family.

Whenever a family divides and another group of individuals attempts to blend as a new family, there are a number of disappointments. Some family members wish it could have been another way. Some remember painful, possibly even abusive incidents. Something has caused a splintering, and the people involved carry the wounds around with them.

The couple themselves must deal with the memories and fears left over from another marriage. If they were rejected, they may live in fear it will happen again. Or they may doubt their ability to love, trust, or be faithful. If they have been mistreated, every raised voice may mean terror.

If only one partner was previously married, he or she may not understand the sensitivity of certain issues or how easily emotions can be triggered. It is important for couples to learn how to sort old baggage from current realities.

There are no guarantees. Some may still need to seek professional help. This course is not a substitute for that help. Be very careful to admit that this session deals with difficult, wrenching issues.

For many, remarriage has been part of God's healing. But at best, this is a gradual process. As you lead the group into this study remind them often: "He heals the brokenhearted and binds up their wounds" (Ps. 147:3).

"To remember the past is to see that we are here today by grace, that we have survived as a gift."

Getting Ready

Scriptures:
Romans 8:29; Philippians 1:6; 3:13, 14, 16; I John 1:9.

1. Have Bibles available for the group to look up the Scriptures for the session.
2. Make photocopies for everyone of "Ghosts from Yesterday" (RS-3A), "Journal Starters" (RS-3B), "Stepping into the Future" (RS-3C), and "When You Need Help" (RS-3D). Two of these resource sheets are for personal use, but you should be familiar with the content.
3. Have blank, lined paper for the activity in Step 3 using a group secretary, and be sure you follow through and make copies of this for the next session.
4. With your pastor and other church staff, develop a list of Christian counselors in your area. Have copies available at the end of the session.

❶ Sorting Yesterday from Today

Objective:
To help couples recognize their need to shed the influence of "yesterday" on "today" (15 minutes).

In *A Room Called Remember*, the contemporary novelist Frederick Buechner [pronounced BEEK-nur] wrote, "Hope stands up to its knees in the past and keeps its eyes on the future. There has never been a time past when God wasn't with us as the strength beyond our strength, the wisdom beyond our wisdom, as whatever it is in our hearts that keeps us human enough at least to get by despite everything in our lives that tends to wither the heart and make us less than human. To remember the past is to see that we are here today by grace, that we have survived as a gift."[1]

Give everyone a copy of "Ghosts from Yesterday" (RS-3A). Ask four volunteers to read one of the stories from the sheet. After all four stories have been read, go back to each story and ask the group these questions:

1. What clues do you hear that someone in the story might be reacting to a situation in the past and letting it influence the way they are relating to their new spouse?

(1. The wife reacts with fear even though her husband has done nothing negative toward her.

2. Upon seeing his wife eating with a co-worker in the cafeteria, the husband immediately assumes the worst without giving his wife a chance to clear up any doubt.

3. The wife assumes her husband is upset with her, but he hasn't shown any anger or irritation.

4. The wife fails to be honest about her preferences, possibly out of fear. Instead of being sensitive to his wife's illness,

The best news of all is that many people who have been broken are now mended, and the grace of God is the glue."

the husband projects this incident to the entire physical relationship.)

2. How could each of the couples see their situation as a gift of grace? (In each case, the couple has an opportunity to apply kindness and healing to old, painful situations. God loves them enough to give them second chances. The more honest and open they are about their emotions, the more they will be able to heal.)

❷ A Place Where People Are Healed

Objective:
To give couples practical help for creating a safe environment in which the healing process can begin (10 minutes).

Healing is a growing process. It takes time, but not just time. There are many elements needed to create an environment in which healing can happen. Author and human development expert Donald Joy believes, "The best news of all is that many people who have been broken are now mended, and the grace of God is the glue."[2] Here are some things he believes are necessary in a healing environment.

Write the following five points on the board or newsprint. Follow each by asking the group members why the suggestion is important.

1. Be realistic. (Denial makes things worse.)

2. Try not to take your partner's response personally. (Mature Christians will understand the person has been hurt by someone else.)

3. Don't alter your behavior to avoid situations that might stir memories or old feelings. (Creating a facade will only delay healing.)

4. Be consistently kind, understanding, and aware. (By giving in to your own moods or weariness you can delay or reverse healing.)

5. When you find yourself feeling something from the past or reacting to an old fear, don't dismiss it. (Consider it an opportunity to receive God's healing and grace.)

When you finish the short discussion, distribute "Journal Starters" (RS-3B). Explain that many people have discovered the healing power in writing out their feelings. Tell them this isn't for use during group time. They should keep it with them and begin a healing journal. These phrases can be used to start each day.

We need clean boundaries between today and yesterday.

❸ A Place for Regrets and Memories

Objective:
To help couples understand what Scripture tells us about our relationship with yesterday (15 minutes).

Again Frederick Buechner suggests, "Because we remember, we have this high and holy hope; that what He has done, He will continue to do, that what He has begun in us and our world, He will in unimaginable ways bring to fullness and fruition."[3]

We need clean boundaries between today and yesterday. The Bible offers four key steps.

Have the group members look up I John 1:9 and Philippians 3:13-16. Say: **These verses contain four keys to developing healthy boundaries between yesterday, today, and tomorrow. Can you find them?**

Give group members a few minutes to find the keys in the passages. Then begin a discussion about what they discovered. Draw attention to these three "keys":

1. I John 1:9—(Key: *Repent and receive forgiveness for past sins.* Guilt and repeated harmful behaviors are likely to invade and damage the new marriage if they have not been squarely faced and dealt with in this biblical fashion.)

2. Philippians 3:13—(Key: *Forget what lies behind.* Experiencing real repentance and forgiveness is the only way one can forget past failures, achievements, self-effort, pains—all the good and bad. When sin is dealt with, we can keep the past where it belongs and neither live on our laurels from yesterday nor dwell on former sins.)

3. Philippians 3:16—(Key: *Recognize what is now.* Hold fast to the present as it is the time you live in—a time for loving, living, growing, experiencing, and becoming more alive to God. Recognize your life as a gift of God and remarriage specifically as a healing gift.)

4. Philippians 3:13b-14—(Key: *Strain toward the future.* It holds promise of healing, second chances, maturity, long life with God. It is God's gift and reason to have hope.)

Paul precedes these encouragements to the Philippians by reminding them: "He who began a good work in you will carry it on to completion until the day of Christ Jesus (1:6)." That good work is knowing Christ and becoming like Him, or as Romans 8:29 calls it, being "conformed to the likeness of Christ."

Read each of the following paragraphs aloud. After each one, ask the group which key (or keys) is reinforced.

Mention that both quotes are from Larry Richards's book, *Remarriage: A Healing Gift from God.*

"God has always had one basic way of dealing with human failure. That way is to come alongside us with the gift of forgiveness and by his healing touch bring that possibility of health and growth."[4]

"We forgive the adulterer in our churches much more quickly than we forgive the woman who has suffered the abandonment of divorce, or the man who has chosen to remarry. We welcome the converted murderer to our pulpits and lionize the reformed purveyor of smut. But somehow we feel it is only right that life-long suffering result for anyone who has been involved in any way in the one unforgivable sin of our day. How strange."[5]

Ask the group: **How can each of us put these keys to use in our lives?** (Accept all answers. Encourage the group to offer concrete suggestions such as: Deal with past sins so that my new blended family does not have to suffer their consequences. Be more forgiving. Pray for new understanding. Focus on the blessings of God. Recognize the past's influence on today and deal with it.)

Your goal here is to help the group internalize and apply the Scriptures to their personal situations. Encourage them to think of something they can actually begin doing.

Appoint someone "secretary" to write down what the group says. Tell them you will make copies of it for them to take home next week.

❹ Letting Go

Objective:
To help couples begin releasing the past and entering the future together with hope (5-20 minutes).

According to David Augsburger in *Caring Enough to Forgive*, there is an important first step before genuine forgiveness—realizing wrongdoing. Whether the confession of sin needs to be made to God, others, or self, each of us must determine according to our situation. However, the principle is the same, and it initiates a process Augsburger describes in his book.[6]

Distribute copies of "Stepping into the Future" (RS-3C), and have group members read each step aloud. If your session is forty-five minutes, the members will have to do the activity at home. In this case, skip to the final paragraph on page 24.

If the session continues, take time to discuss "Stepping into the Future" (RS-3C). Ask the group at which point in the

Drop demands for ironclad guarantees of no more pain or misbehavior; this opens the promise of the future.

process forgiveness begins to influence the way they can relate to others. (Step 3 is the hurdle, Steps 4 and 5 are both acts of forgiveness. In Step 3, forgiveness has been activated.) If time allows, ask participants to share which of these steps they find most difficult, personally. Also discuss how each step applies to oneself and others.

Step 1. Recognize the worth of the offender, regardless of the wrong done. (God created us, and we find our worth in Him, not in our own worthiness. We all have worth to God, even though we make mistakes.)

Step 2. Cancel demands on the past by admitting it is unchangeable. (We can't change what we did or what others did, so we must move on.)

Step 3. Work through anger to the point of trusting others and risking again. (If no one mentions it, point out that this step is gradual, it doesn't just happen. As Christians, we can begin to believe in ourselves and in God's work in us. We must stop punishing ourselves.) If you have non-Christians in your group, this may be a good time to share the Gospel or answer any questions about God's forgiveness.

Step 4. Drop demands for ironclad guarantees of no more pain or misbehavior; this opens the promise of the future. (We must accept our limits and the fact that we might make a mistake again. Others will probably disappoint us also. Face reality. The future can be filled with blessing, even though it isn't perfect.)

Step 5. Connect with others, feel genuine love and forgiveness; this opens the potential of healthy relationships again. (Make commitments to love. Give others the chance to love us. Be willing to trust and love others even though we accept that they aren't perfect.)

Before closing, mention that sometimes these issues are so difficult that group members may not know how to handle them on their own. They will need wisdom from God, but they may also need professional help. Pass out copies of "When You Need Help" (RS-3D) and the list of Christian counselors you developed with your church staff. Encourage them to read it soon. Close in prayer, asking God to help every person move from the pain of yesterday into the bright promise of forgiveness and restoration. You may want to read the following promise from God's word out loud: **"He heals the brokenhearted and binds up their wounds"** (Ps. 147:3).

H e heals the brokenhearted and binds up their wounds."

Notes:

1. Frederick Buechner, *A Room Called Remember* (San Francisco: Harper and Row, 1984), p. 46.
2. Donald Joy, *Rebonding: Preventing and Restoring Damaged Relationships* (Waco, Tex.: Word, 1986), p. 136.
3. Frederick Buechner, *Telling Secrets* (New York: Harper Collins, 1991), p. 33.
4. Larry Richards, *Remarriage: A Healing Gift from God* (Waco, Tex.: Word Books, 1981), p. 46.
5. Ibid.
6. David Augsburger, *Caring Enough to Forgive* (Ventura, Calif.: Regal Books, 1981), p. 16.

The Dreaded Ex

4

Session Aim:
To give parents positive suggestions for managing their relationships with former spouses, their children's biological parents.

A child is born to two parents and loves both. When a family divides, the children usually feel deeply and painfully the loss of one parent from their everyday lives.

For the remarried couple, life is probably better than it has been in a long time, but that's not always true for their children. A stepparent will never take the place of a biological parent or at least what the biological parent should have been to the child. For this reason, it's important for custodial and non-custodial parents to work together at providing children with the presence, love, and support of both birth parents.

Of course, there are rare exceptions. If a child has been abused by his or her non-custodial parent, contact may need to be limited or prohibited, but those are extreme cases.

In most situations when a custodial parent doesn't want an ex-spouse involved in a child's life it is because of offenses against the adult, not the child. Often a person who has been abandoned for a new lover or who was once married to an alcoholic will feel this way. Helping these parents see that their child needs a relationship with a less than ideal parent is not an easy matter.

It's important for parents to work together at providing children with the presence, love, and support of both birth parents.

Getting Ready

Scripture:
Romans 12:18; II Corinthians 13:11; Proverbs 2:10, 11; James 1:5; 3:17.

1. Have enough index cards, blank paper, and Bibles for the whole group.
2. Prepare copies of "Enabling Communication" (RS-4A, "Problems and More Problems" (RS-4B), and the "Actions to Be Taken" list developed in Step 3 of Session 3 for each participant. Three-hole punch these sheets if your group members are compiling notebooks.
3. Determine in advance how many and which of the problems from "Problems and More Problems" (RS-4B) you will use. Highlight or mark the ones you select for the session.
4. If you wish a group member to read the excerpt from an issue of "Stepfamilies" newsletter in Step 1, photocopy it for ease of use during the session.

❶ About the Ex

Objective:
To encourage individuals to think about their relationships with their ex-spouses and how they impact their children (10-20 minutes).

After welcoming the group, distribute copies of the "Action to Be Taken" list from Session 3. Give an opportunity for volunteers to briefly share their successes or frustrations as they attempted to follow through on their intentions.

Pass out index cards and ask everyone to write down a specific problem they have had with an ex-spouse. Encourage the people to keep it simple and not to write their names on their cards. Gather these to use at the end of the session.

Next, either ask a volunteer to read or read aloud the following excerpt from a true story that was printed in an issue of "Stepfamilies" newsletter. Provide paper for each group member to make notes about how the woman in the story reacts to her situation in two ways: EMOTIONS and ACTIONS. Have them label the paper accordingly.

> **At the time of our family's deterioration, I had been the sole support for my children. . . . It was I who stayed up with them in consoling them when their father didn't come home at night. I was the one who worked hard at keeping things as stable as possible.**
>
> **As time passed and I adjusted to single parenthood, I continued, with pride, making certain that my children's physical, emotional, and spiritual needs were being met. . . . They were better off with me, because I was better at meeting their needs. In fact, I gave myself another pat on the back for all**

Problems develop for children when their parents don't love unconditionally.

the times I bit my tongue and never bad-mouthed their father to them.

When the man of my dreams came into the picture, I was certain my children would have the wonderful father figure they never had. To my amazement they seemed to miss their dad even more. . . . A stepdad wouldn't do.[1]

After reading the story, give the group a few minutes to talk about their own insights. When leading the discussion, try to make these points.

EMOTIONS—(The writer seems to have felt anger, rejection, bitterness, and confusion over what happened after she remarried.)

ACTIONS—(She worked hard to provide for her children. She supported the children's relationship with their father, at least on the surface.)

Ask: **Is any expectation mentioned in the story that might have caused problems in the remarriage?** (Note that she said the children would now have a wonderful father figure. She expected a certain relationship to exist between her new husband and children.)

Ask: **How you would feel if you were in this woman's situation?**

If you have an hour-long session, provide time for the group members to share how their relationships with their ex-spouses impact their children.

---

❷ For the Children

Objective:
To help remarried couples find ways to communicate and behave peaceably with the former spouse for the sake of their children (15 minutes).

Every one of us wants what is best for our children. Relationships between two divorced parents are complex and, by nature, filled with conflict. Ann M. Corley, the woman whose story we read earlier, writes, "Reflecting back over the years, I could see that all I did was out of love for my children. But was it unconditional love?"

Problems develop for children when their parents don't love unconditionally. Corley suggests that putting children in a tug-of-war between parents and dividing the children's loyalties is one demonstration of conditional love. "Did I somehow expect unconditional loyalty in return? Was I placing my children in a tug-of-war of emotions, expecting them to always be on my side of the ropes?"

On the board or newsprint, create two columns. Label one "unconditional love" and the other "conditional love." Ask: **Can you think of things divorced parents might say or do that demonstrate each of these?** Begin with conditional, then contrast it as you create the other list. If these aren't on the list, include them:

Conditional—(Asking children to make choices between spending time with parents; using children as a tool to manipulate or hurt the ex-spouse; keeping biological parent away from children's events and activities; not allowing children to talk about other parent.)

Unconditional—(Giving children freedom to spend as much time with their parent as they appear to need; not forcing them to accept a new stepparent; allowing, accepting, and encouraging their loving feelings for the other parent; not forcing your unpleasant memories on children.)

Protecting our children from having to choose between parents is one of the most difficult things we must do. It requires us to act not only like real adults, but to put selfishness aside for the good of the children. What are the keys to being able to do this? (It only works when we know, deep down, that our children will be better off if they have a healthy relationship with their biological parent. It requires facing our failures in this area regularly and learning to forgive others and ourselves.)

Pass out "Enabling Communication" (RS-4A). This is a list of several suggestions for how to make communications between biological parents less stressful. Give the group a few minutes to go over the list and check off those that would be most helpful for them to try.

Keeping your time limit in mind, give participants an opportunity to comment or add to the list. If possible, include the following comments about each item.

Item 1—(The agenda is a tool to keep discussion on track. This is especially important for relationships that are emotionally charged.)

Item 2—(Be careful that you don't demand or expect the other parent to comply with your rules. This will meet with resistance. Both of you must be flexible.)

Item 3—(This is important if your spouse feels threatened by your previous marriage or concerned about your welfare.)

Item 4—(This also acts as an agreement and helps avoid conflict. It provides a basis for expectations and accountability.)

Items 5 and 6—(Acknowledge that these take extra effort but parents who do them find they work out well.)

Item 7—(Some parents will find this idea hard to accept. Encourage them to view it as a way of loving their children unconditionally. Remind them that they are doing this for the children, not for their ex-spouses.)

❸ Living Wisely in Peace

Objective:
To help parents live at peace with their former spouses in response to the biblical calling. (15-20 minutes).

On the board write, "We are called to peace" and "We are called to wisdom." Then under each, write the selected Bible reference and ask for a volunteer to look up each and read it out loud. For each passage ask: **What does this mean in relationship to a former spouse?**

We are called to peace.
Romans 12:18—(It is our responsibility to do everything possible to keep the peace.)
II Corinthians 13:11—(Try to agree. Don't hold out for the right to have your own opinion for it's own sake. Seek peace.)

We are called to wisdom.
Proverbs 2:10, 11—(Trying to understand the other person's perspective and behaving in a discreet fashion is wise and will protect us from conflict.)
James 1:5—(God is the source of all wisdom and is eager to share it with us.)

Conclude this discussion by opening your Bible to James 3:17 and saying: **Wisdom and peace are intricately linked in Scripture. James 3:17 says this, "the wisdom that comes from heaven is first of all pure; then peace-loving, considerate, submissive, full of mercy and good fruit, impartial and sincere."**

Pass out "Problems and More Problems" (RS-4B). This sheet has several hypothetical situations on it. Pick out as many as you have time for (reserving five minutes for Step 4) and discuss the best way to resolve the issue within the biblical guidelines of peace and wisdom.

Put the responsibility on someone who can do something about it.

Problem 1: *Because Timmy stayed up late watching television while overnight at his mother's house, he didn't study for his test and fell asleep in math class Monday morning.*

(Present the problem to your child's mother. "I know how concerned you are that Timmy do well in school. His teacher called today and said he fell asleep in class and had not studied for his test. Would you talk to him about it?"

Why does this work? It puts the responsibility on someone who can do something about it. You can't make Timmy study at his mother's house. You can't even make his mother encourage Timmy to study. But it's possible that she didn't know about the test. It's possible that she fell asleep, and Timmy just stayed up. Since you don't know the whole situation, give it back to the one who can do something about it.)

Problem 2: *Your ex-husband has agreed to return the children to your house Christmas Eve by 8 P.M. He calls at 10:30 P.M. and says his mother would like to keep the children overnight and will bring them home in the morning.* (Refer to the written schedule you worked out and that your plans have been made according to it; suggest his mother call you to make other plans; and apologize for inconvenience it may cause.)

Problem 3: *Julie is seven years old and lives with her mom. Her mother insists she go to bed at 8 P.M. One night she responded with, "Dad lets me stay up until 10."* (Talk directly with her dad and ask without accusing. One mom did this and the dad laughingly said, "No, she goes to bed at 8 P.M. here too.")

Problem 4: *Twelve-year-old Michael tells you his mother has a different man spending the weekend with them than she did last month. He asks, "Why can't I be alone with Mom?"* (Different moral standards present unique problems. Suggest that Michael ask his mother about her actions. Tell him you don't know why she's doing what she's doing. Tell your ex-spouse that you told Michael to talk to her about it because he expressed concern. It is important that you clearly state God's standard without condemning or criticizing Michael's mother. If these things begin impacting your child's behavior, you will need to express concern over the child's behavior and seek professional help.)

Problem 5: *Laticia is disappointed when her father doesn't show up for a school play. You don't recall that anyone thought to call him about it.* (After apologizing, decide who will make the calls in the future and stick to it.)

❹ Stepping toward Peace

Objective:
To focus on actual problems or situations concerning a former spouse and brainstorm possible peaceful solutions (5 minutes).

Tell participants you're going to read the cards they filled out at the beginning of the session. Suggest they jot down any solutions or insights offered from the group.

Read the problems from the index cards participants filled out at the beginning of the session. Ask the group to briefly brainstorm about each one. Encourage them to think quickly and keep their suggestions within the biblical guidelines of peacemaking. Keep this very short and to the point.

Close by praying for God's help when parents must relate to ex-spouses in painful, complicated situations. Ask that God remind each person to work for peace and act wisely.

Notes:

1. Ann M. Corley, "Co-Parenting: a Difficult Concept for Stepfamilies to Develop," *Stepfamilies: Providing Education and Support,* Volume 13, Number 2, Summer 1993, p. 5.

Who's the Boss?

5

Session Aim:
To help couples identify family power struggles and understand the nature of godly leadership and mutual submission within the family.

The issue of authority is especially important in stepfamilies. Many second marriages end, at least in part, because of disagreements over children. It is likely that parental authority will be questioned by stepchildren.

A solid understanding of biblical leadership and a biblical approach to mutual submission contribute to an environment of peace. Biblical leadership balances authority with service and mercy. Mutual submission begins by listening carefully to the other person and seriously considering the possibility that he or she is right. Consideration for the other person's point of view encourages godly leadership and submission.

The appropriate climate for parents to raise children in is one where husband and wife are submitted to each other in the spirit of Ephesians 5:21-33.

According to Gilbert Bilezikian, author, leader in Willow Creek Community Church, and biblical studies professor at Wheaton College, "In the New Testament, the command to obey is given to children and slaves (Eph. 6:5; Col. 3:20, 22), never to husbands or wives. . . . This mutuality in equality is reflected in the fact that both husband and wife have a responsibility of leadership in the home. . . . Children are made accountable to both parents.

"A husband and wife locked in a power struggle will have no more credibility as leaders to their children than a mother who demands obedience from her children while she is herself treated as a child."[1]

*T*he appropriate climate for raising children in is one where husband and wife are submitted to each other in the spirit of Christ.

Getting Ready

Scriptures:
Genesis 1:27, 28; Ephesians 5:22-33; I Corinthians 11:3; Mark 9:35; Matthew 18:3, 4; 20:25-28.

1. Prepare copies of "Playing with Power" (RS-5A), and "Leadership Turned Upside Down" (RS-5B). Decide whether you'll cut apart the sections of RS-5B or have group members do so. Three-hole punch if necessary.
2. Make a copy of the statements in Step 1 for those who wish to review their reactions. Don't pass this out, but make it available.
3. The activities in Step 1 will require space to move around. Decide if you need to rearrange furniture or change lighting to accommodate this session.

❶ Noting the Powers That Be

Objective:
To give participants an opportunity to interact with the subject of authority and note the range of differences among themselves (5-10 minutes).

Acknowledge that this session will delve into a controversial and difficult realm, the issue of power and authority in the family. Accept that some group members may struggle with some of the ideas to be discussed.

To reveal the variety of convictions, have the group indicate their understanding of leadership in the home by moving to different positions in the room. Designate one end for "I agree" and the other end for "I disagree": The center of the room will be neutral or "I don't know what I think yet."

Explain that as you read a statement, group members should immediately go to the location that best represents their opinion. Say: **Some of these statements are clear-cut, and some are controversial. With some statements, you'll partially agree or partially disagree. If so, place yourself accordingly. Try to respond honestly even if you are standing alone! The purpose of this activity is for you to examine your own personal convictions.**

Allow no more than thirty seconds for people to consider each statement before moving on to the next one.

1. **Children should obey their parents immediately and without question.**
2. **Wives shouldn't disagree with their husbands.**
3. **Children should obey their father.**
4. **Children should obey their mother.**
5. **A child who questions the authority of a stepparent is rebellious.**
6. **Submission indicates inferiority or weakness.**
7. **Christians should not seek positions of authority over others.**

8. **Godly leaders have the right to do things their own way.**
9. **The husband should be the decision maker.**
10. **Stepparents should have the same kind of parental authority as biological parents.**

When all statements have been read, have group members sit down and think about what they have just experienced. Discuss their reactions for a few minutes, focusing on their feelings.

❷ Playing with Power

Objective:
To help couples identify destructive power struggles in their own families (15-20 minutes).

Read the following quote from the *Stepfamilies* newsletter:

Early in remarriage, the most successful step-parent-stepchild relationships are those where the stepparent focuses first on the development of a warm, friendly interaction style with the stepchild. Once a foundation of mutual respect and affection is established, stepparents who then attempt to assume a disciplinarian role are less likely to meet with resentment from the stepchild. . . . Parenting behaviors that include high levels of warmth, support, and control are associated with positive child outcomes in first-marriage families. [But initially] this pattern of parenting behaviors known as authoritative parenting doesn't [always] have the same positive outcome in stepfamilies.[2]

In other words, it is wise to start slow when establishing authority as a stepparent.

Divide the parents into three groups, separating couples and mixing men and women. Designate each group as number 1, 2, or 3.

Give everyone a copy of "Playing with Power" (RS-5A). Groups will roleplay the situations assigned by number. Encourage them to keep these roleplays short and honest. Allow a few minutes for groups to assign parts and prepare. Have each group "perform" for the other two groups.

Be alert to the best time to end the roleplay. When it is clear that someone is asserting power that elicits a negative response, end the scene. After each roleplay, encourage the groups to make a few notes about their own responses or how

"Jesus turned upside down the disciples' worldly, pagan view of community organization as a pyramid of power."

they might react in a similar situation.

Say: **Identifying how we assert power in relationships is a very personal thing. Take a few minutes to think of any situations in your family when you or your spouse asserted power inappropriately. List these situations on the back of your resource sheet.**

❸ A Biblical Model

Objective:
To help couples better understand the biblical concept of leadership and mutual submission (15 minutes).

Distribute copies of "Leadership Turned Upside Down" (RS-5B). Ask someone to write the Scripture references and "key words" on the board or newsprint as you go over the resource sheet.

Say: **Gilbert Bilezikian, professor of Biblical Studies at Wheaton College and author of** *Beyond Sex Roles* **explains: "Jesus turned upside down the disciples' worldly, pagan view of community organization as a pyramid of power. He showed them that greatness was achieved in Christian communities by serving at the very bottom."**[3]

Today we still have trouble understanding the biblical model of leadership. As a group read each Scripture passage aloud and identify the key words.

Genesis 1:27, 28—(Rule over)
Mark 9:35—(Wants to be first)
Matthew 18:3 —(Is the greatest)
Matthew 20:25-28—(Exercise authority)

Have group members jot down the meaning of the key words according to the world's view and the new meaning given by Jesus. After a few minutes, open it up for discussion.

Ask the group to share their opinions of how biblical sayings on power or authority were "upside down" compared to the typical worldly view.

For each passage, stress the following points if they aren't brought up.

Genesis 1:27, 28—(The text is filled with the concept of organization, yet no hierarchical organization is indicated between man and woman as it is concerning humans over animals. The man and woman's relationship was one of mutuality, and supremacy of one or the other was not God's intention. Note in Genesis 3:16 that it was a result of sin that the woman was told that her husband would "rule

Jesus says being first means being last. It means putting others before yourself.

over" her. References to the *head*ship of the husband [I Corinthians 11:3; Ephesians 5:23] were not intended as licenses to husbands to throw their weight around. Instead they were meant to signify sacrificial servant-leadership [Eph. 5:25].)

Note that Ephesians 5:22 clearly reveals that God intends couples to demonstrate mutual respect and submission. Refer to the session introduction for further discussion on the nature of mutual submission.

Mark 9:35—(Jesus says being first means being last. It means putting others before yourself.)

Matthew 18:3, 4—(Children are viewed as powerless, dependent, and helpless. Jesus said those considered the greatest must become like children.)

Matthew 20:25-28—(The matter discussed here is who will be the leader and make decisions. The social values of the day indicated that one person had to have the power of final decision. In verse 26, Jesus told the disciples that it's not to be so among them. Their values were not to be the values of the social world around them.)

❹ What Kind of Leader Will You Be?

Objective:
To help couples focus on what kind of leadership they are using in their homes (10-15 minutes).

The issues just addressed in the study section may appear radically different from what some group members have heard about leadership. To help them process this information and to lighten things up, do the next activity.

Explain that the entire group is going to write a classified ad for Christians to lead blended families in a biblical style.

Begin by having the group come up with a list of qualifications of a godly leader. List these on the board. (The list should include words like this: humility, servant's attitude, submission, team player, loving, unselfish, willing to be last, not seeking power.)

After a few minutes, have the group write their ad using words from the list. Have fun with this exercise, but keep close watch on your time. Make sure to leave five or ten minutes for the closing personal activity. Begin by writing on poster board or newsprint: **Wanted—Men and Women to Lead Blended Families . . .**

Have group members refer to the situations they recorded

Ask God to help all parents and stepparents to understand their roles as servant-leaders living under the reign of Christ.

on the back of RS-5A. Encourage them to prayerfully consider how they have expressed leadership in their home. Call attention to the phrase in Matthew 20:26: "Not so with you." Allow a few minutes of quiet for review of the biblical view of leadership and any notes they have taken, as well as prayer for their unique situations.

Conclude by having each couple write a short prayer for themselves as leaders in their families. Give them two or three minutes to complete this. Ask those who are willing to share their prayers. Close the group prayer time by asking God to help all parents and stepparents to understand their roles as servant-leaders living under the reign and rule of Jesus Christ.

Notes:

1. Gilbert Bilezikian, *Beyond Sex Roles* (Grand Rapids, Mich., Baker, 1985), 167-172.
2. Kay Pasley, David Dollahite, Marilyn Ihinger-Tallman, "Researcher's Corner," *Stepfamilies: Providing Education and Support*, Volume 13, Number 2, Summer 1993, 10.
3. Bilezikian, 106-115.

Understanding and Handling Conflict

6

Session Aim:
To teach couples practical, workable skills for healthy and productive conflict resolution.

At times, it seems like a blended family is a breeding ground for conflict. Yet the experts say that *all* relationships experience conflict. Those of us who live with the reality of stepparenting sometimes think conflict is a way of life unique to us.

Any approach to resolving conflict must begin by acknowledging that blended families can *expect* conflict. Patricia Papernow wrote a chapter for a manual for the Stepfamily Association of America. In it, she explores the various stages stepfamilies can expect to go through.

"After the fantasy phase comes the reality phase, and it can be a shock. The original dreams of unified family life are destroyed and there's no easy substitute. All the family members feel they have lost something."[1]

Most blended families discover this is when conflict culminates. It's common for families to require professional help. Families should be encouraged to view it as wise and courageous when they reach out for the help their family critically needs. They should also be advised that it takes time for relationships to strengthen in the new family. Patience is a much needed virtue in blended families.

These are difficult issues. It should be stressed that answers presented in these sessions are not intended to replace the guidance of a trained professional.

Begin by acknowledging that blended families can expect conflict.

Getting Ready

Scriptures:
I Corinthians 10:31—11:1; Matthew 7:3-5; Lamentations 3:40; Galatians 6:1, 4, 5; Matthew 18:15; Ephesians 4:15, 29; Colossians 3:12-15; Luke 6:27-33, 38; Proverbs 9:11.

1. Prepare enough copies of "Your Own Style" (RS-6A), "Stepping toward Peace" (RS-6B), "Communication Checklist" (RS-6C), and "Working toward Resolution" (RS-6D) for everyone. Be sure to note which of these are for group use and which are for personal use. Have extra copies of RS-6D available. Three-hole punch if necessary.
2. Make a poster entitled, "Overlook an Offense When . . ." (see Step 4 for the four guidelines). Use large lettering on plain white poster board and keep it turned away from the group until time to use it.
3. You will need these supplies: lined paper, pens or pencils, Bibles, newsprint or board to write on.

❶ Identifying Conflict

Objective:
To help couples identify areas of conflict within their families (5-10 minutes).

After welcoming the group, tell them you'll begin with a story:

> **If you knew Jack well, you would notice he was nervous while singing his first solo in freshman choir. Glen, his stepfather knew. They had worked together for weeks on the piano to make sure every pitch sounded just right. Glen had never felt more proud than he did at that moment. He squeezed his wife's hand and dabbed at a proud tear on her cheek.**
>
> **A few rows ahead of them sat Jack's biological father.**
>
> **Jack had been nervous about inviting him, because "sometimes he's such a perfectionist." Glen understood how it feels to be left out of your own children's lives. Sometimes it happened with his children. So, he encouraged Jack to call his father.**
>
> **When the song was over, the audience applause seemed to melt Jack's apprehension into a wide grin. Glen cheered louder than most. Jack smoothed the tie they had picked out together. *Talented and handsome, that's my boy*, Glen thought. He felt sudden gratitude to his new bride for the gift of his stepson.**
>
> **Jack bounded off the stage then. His long legs carried him to his father's side. Glen and Jack's mother walked toward them. Jack took his mother's**

hand and his father's. His gaze never met Glen's eager, beaming face. The boy pulled his parents away to meet his choir director and have a glass of punch.

Meanwhile, Glen watched from a distance and talked to strangers. He waited to drive Jack and his mother home.

Ask: **What potential for conflict exists in this situation? Who might be angry at whom?** (Possible answers— Glen at stepson Jack, Glen at his wife, Mother at son, Jack at everyone, etc.) Keep the discussion short and make the point that every person in it might have reason, in his or her own mind, for being upset.

If time allows, pass out lined sheets of paper. Ask participants to write briefly about a situation in which their own family is experiencing conflict. Hold these to use in Step 5.

❷ Understanding Conflict Resolution

Objective:
To help couples understand their personal style of approaching conflict and how it impacts conflict resolution (10 minutes).

How we view conflict determines our response, writes Ken Sande in *The Peacemaker*.

The way we look at conflict strongly influences the way we respond to it. For example, people who believe that conflict is wrong . . . are uncomfortable with personal differences of any kind. . . . On the other hand, people who see conflict as an inconvenience want to get through it as quickly as possible. . . . There are people who view conflict as a contest. They see it as an opportunity to assert their rights.[2]

Pass out copies of "Your Own Style" (RS-6A). Quickly read over each description of conflict management style listed.

Say: **According to Ken Sande, Executive Director of the Christian Conciliation Service, there are strengths and difficulties with each of these style. Let's try to identify these styles in our own experience.**

Give the group a few minutes to complete the resource sheet, but don't get bogged down here. It's okay if they can't think of someone for each type. The most important thing is that they recognize their own style.

❸ Biblical Principles of Conflict Resolution

Objective:
To discuss biblical principles for guiding conflict resolution and help the couples immediately apply these principles (15 minutes).

Pass out "Stepping toward Peace" (RS-6B). Mention that in *The Peacemaker*, Ken Sande proposes a four-principled approach to resolving conflict.[3] After taking time to personally study the Scripture lesson for each principle, go over it together in the group. If you prefer to have group members study the passages in a group, break them into two or three small groups.

Ask participants to share the questions and actions they wrote down or thought of in response to the text. Their answers will vary. Remember, there is no right or wrong answer here. Try to guide them according to the suggestions that follow each passage as suggested below.

Principle 1: Glorify God
I Corinthians 10:31—11:1

(How can I please and honor God in this situation? What would Jesus do? Am I motivated by selfish intentions, or am I concerned with honoring God?)

Principle 2: Get the log out of my own eye
Matthew 7:3-5; Lamentations 3:40; Galatians 6:4, 5

(How have I contributed to the conflict? What can I do to help resolve this? Do I need to confess something? Am I over-eager to protect my own rights?)

Principle 3: Go and show your brother his fault
Galatians 6:1; Matthew 18:15; Ephesians 4:15, 29

(How can I help others understand their contribution to this conflict? Why do I feel hurt and who should I talk to about this? Do I want to confront to prove my point or because I'm concerned about the other person? Can I express this without sounding demanding?)

You can add at this point that Sande says this step is best handled only when you have received guidance about what happens next. Talk to someone who can be trusted. Ask if your perspective seems right. Be open to the possibility that your motivations for wanting confrontation might not be pure.

Principle 4: Go and be reconciled
Colossians 3:12-15; Luke 6:27-33, 38

(How can I forgive and encourage a reasonable solution? Have I been resistant to forgiving? Have I been resistant to apologizing? What actions do I need to take to demonstrate willingness to forgive? What actions can I take to show I still care? Am I willing to move on, without drawing anything from the past into today, or demanding reassurances?)

❹ When and How to Fight

Objective:
To present options to conflict and, since all conflict cannot be avoided, communication skills that will help families grow toward unity (10-15 minutes).

Say this: **While often unpleasant, conflict is an opportunity to honor God and grow as a family and a person.**

Sometimes it is appropriate to overlook an offense. Proverbs 19:11 teaches us this. Remember, God who works for the best of His children, doesn't deal harshly with us each time we sin. Are we willing to treat others the same way?

For the stepfamily, where conflict is inevitable, it is important to learn early that saving the battles for what really matters makes life much easier. Discover what you can live with.

1. The offense hasn't created a wall between you and another person.
2. It hasn't caused you to feel different about the other person.
3. It hasn't hurt you, the other person, or anyone else.
4. You are able to "cast it into the sea of forgetfulness" and not bring it up at a later date.

Acknowledge that it is not always possible, or desirable, to overlook an offense. When that's the case, how we confront, communicate, and resolve the situation is crucial.

Communication is more than talking to one another. To really communicate, listening is important. Pass out copies of "Communication Checklist" (RS-6C).

One by one go through the list, allowing the group to discuss and react. Do not get involved in a debate about the "rights" and "wrongs" of each one. Instead, encourage them to discuss how they feel about each, the difficulty or benefit of it, etc. Keep the discussion focused on the resource sheet and remember your time limit.

End the discussion by saying something such as: **We have to admit that conflict can become emotional. Experts such as Ken Sande suggest that rather than responding emotionally, we try asking for more clarification or information. In other words, keep the other person talking. What can we say that will accomplish this?**

Ask a volunteer to write responses on the board. Suggest

that group members all take notes. Be sure to include these suggestions: ("Why do you feel this is true?" "Can you help me understand?" "What else do you think?" "Could you give me an example?" "Is there anything you'd like to clarify?")

❺ Keep the Goal in Sight

Objective:
To help stepparents understand the importance of staying focused on resolution as an honest goal when conflict happens (5-10 minutes).

Pass out "Working toward Resolution" (RS-6D). Note that the top section can be used to set goals for conflict resolution. Then, draw group members' attention to the bottom section of the work sheet and say: **Personal interest is usually involved when conflict arises. By using this section to evaluate those personal interests, we can determine whether or not that personal interest is reasonable, godly, and worthwhile.**

Challenge group members to apply this to a conflict they are now experiencing. If they wrote out a family conflict at the beginning of the session, prayerfully use the work sheet to plan a resolution.

Give them a few minutes to do this. If you are working with the shorter session, participants may only make a start. As you close, encourage them to finish the work sheet on their own. Close in prayer asking God to help each person learn to manage conflict in ways that bring honor to Him.

Notes:

1. Barbara Kantrowitz and Pat Wingert, "Step by Step: Who Will We Be?" *Newsweek* Special Issue Winter/Spring, Volume 114, 1990, p. 34.
2. Ken Sande, *The Peacemaker* (Grand Rapids, Mich.: Baker, 1991), pp. 16-18.
3. Ibid, pp. 8, 9.

Parental Authority and Discipline

7

Session Aim:
To help blended family parents understand the limits and difficulties of stepparent authority.

Stepchildren are almost always resistant to stepparent authority. The reasons are many and complex. Even so, it's vital to the health of the family and remarried couple that a strong relationship develop between stepparent and stepchild.

According to Emily and John Visher, founders of the Stepfamily Association of America and recognized researchers in the stepfamily area, "Even though there is marital satisfaction, research is indicating that often [step] families do not stay together when positive stepparent/stepchild relationships are not developed. Dynamically, this is quite different from first marriages."[1]

Remarried couples get tired of hearing how different their situation is from that of first marriages. It's a message that sometimes overwhelms them with despair. This session will give couples the information they need to defeat this kind of despair and frustration.

For many years, because professionals weren't interested in blended families, stepfamilies were on their own in developing parenting strategies. This is changing. Still, what research reveals can be discouraging for stepfamilies. It is becoming obvious that blended families have to work very hard to accomplish unity.

When the facts are challenging, it's tempting to avoid them. However, for the stepfamily, survival depends on facing reality and handling it with prayer, love, wisdom, and patience.

Acknowledge that stepparenting is a mixed bag of ups and downs.

Getting Ready

Scriptures:
Proverbs 10:17; Ephesians
6:4; Hebrews 12:5, 6.

1. Make a poster with the closing prayer printed on it in large, easy to read letters (see page). Black lettering on white poster board will work best.
2. Bring two items such as bells for the group to use as a signal in the game played in Step 2, "For Your Information." Review the questions ahead of time and decide which you will use. Optional: small prize (mints or gum) for each winning team member.
3. Prepare copies of "Stepparent Quiz Bowl" (RS-7A), "Weighing Your Shoulds" (RS-7B), "Tips for Stepparents" (RS-7C), and two copies per participant of "The Cycle of Anger" (RS-7C). Use a three-hole punch if needed.
4. Have available newsprint or board, extra Bibles, poster board, pens, pencils.

❶ The Beautiful and Beastly Reality

Objective:
To allow stepparents to talk about the pleasures and pains of stepparenting (5 minutes). NOTE: If you're working with a shorter session, you may begin with Step 2.

Ask group members to reflect over the last week with their stepchildren. Suggest they do this exercise: shut their eyes and picture Monday morning, or their first contact with the children. Tell them to hold that image in their mind until it's clear and they can remember how they felt.

Then they should play back the week, as if it's on a video in their mind. Tell them to do this and then open their eyes. When group members have opened their eyes, ask them to describe the week in one sentence.

Be sure everyone who wants to talk has a chance, but remember your time limit. Close this segment by acknowledging that stepparenting is a mixed bag of ups and downs.

❷ For Your Information

Objective:
To present research to stepparents that will help them understand the challenges and reality of their own situations (10 minutes).

Divide the group into two equal-sized teams. If teams are uneven, have someone be the timekeeper. Tell them you're going to play "Stepparent Quiz Bowl." Give each side a bell to ring or something to bang on the table when they have an answer to the question (pans and spoons will work too). The team that signals first has a chance to answer the question. If they're wrong, the question is thrown out.

One by one, read aloud the questions on "Stepparent Quiz Bowl" (RS-7A). Give teams five to ten seconds to respond before providing the answer. It isn't necessary to present all the questions if time is short. If you have extra time, ask the team that answers correctly to explain their answer.

After the game, pass out copies of RS-7A to each group member. Ask if they were surprised by any of the information. Also, ask how they feel about what they have learned. Encourage them to admit that stepparenting is one of the most challenging roles any person can accept.

❸ From the Child's Perspective

Objective:
To help the stepparent understand the obstacles, fears, and difficulties faced by children in stepfamilies (10 minutes—you may skip to the next step if you are working with a shorter time frame).

Say: **Author William Coleman grew up with a stepmother. As a speaker on stepparent topics he says, "Children in stepfamilies face enormous issues. If they look to traditional families to find the answers, they will only be bewildered, because stepfamilies are different. Stepfamilies have great strengths, but they are not biological families. We only hurt children if we expect them to pretend nothing has happened."[2]**

According to researchers Emily and John Visher, "We think of issues for children in stepfamilies as being in three general categories, the three L's—loss, loyalty and lack of control."[3]

Write these three categories—Loss, Loyalty, Lack of Control—on the board or across the top of newsprint. Ask: **Within these categories, what major changes do children experience when a parent remarries?** If participants don't mention the following, add them to the list.

- Change in household composition (For example, one day you're an only child and then you have new siblings)
- Reconciliation fantasy completely destroyed
- More need to share generally—money, space, time
- More need to share their parent (Some children feel that their stepparent is guilty of "parent theft.")
- Loss of former role and relationship with single parent
- Split loyalties between parent and stepparent of same gender
- Move to different house or neighborhood (Means new school, new friends, new neighbors, etc.)

Keep this exercise to a few minutes. Ask: **How would you feel if all of this had happened to you and you were personally powerless to do anything about it?** (Expect responses such as: confused, bitter, angry, resentful, withdrawn, uncooperative, frightened, hopeless.)

*O**ur job as parents is to empower our children to become mature."*

End this section by quoting the Vishers, **"At the time of the remarriage we find that the emotions of the adults and of the children are often as far apart as they ever will be. The adults are on a pink cloud of anticipation, while the children, in marked contrast, are unhappy [that] they are faced with many losses."**[4]

❹ Top Challenge, Top Problem— Discipline

Objective:
To understand the biblical concept of discipline and help stepparents understand the purposes of appropriate discipline (15 minutes).

We all know that children need discipline. It is important to understand why and how. Ask volunteers to read aloud the following passages of Scripture. Tell the group to think about what the passages tell us concerning desired *results* of discipline and *appropriate* discipline.

Proverbs 10:17
Ephesians 6:4
Hebrews 12:5, 6

Write each Scripture reference on the board as they are read aloud. List participants' responses very briefly under each passage. Be sure the following points are included.

Proverbs 10:17—(discipline should develop wisdom and understanding in those who learn from it)
Ephesians 6:4—(discipline shouldn't exasperate or frustrate children)
Hebrews 12:5, 6—(discipline should be loving)

After a short discussion say: **Discipline is only part of the process of raising children. The entire goal of parenthood should be kept in mind when disciplining. According to noted Christian psychologist and author Norman Wright, "Our job as parents is to empower our children to become mature . . . to assist our children in moving from dependence on us, to semi-dependence, to independence from us and dependence on God, which is a true reflection of maturity."**[5]

Pass out copies of "Weighing Your Shoulds" (RS-7B). Go over the directions before giving the group a few minutes to work on the resource sheet individually.

❺ Stepparent Distinctives

Objective:

To give stepparents suggestions for their appropriate involvement in disciplining stepchildren (10 minutes).

Say: **According to research published in** *Stepfamilies* **newsletter, ". . . early in remarriage good marital adjustment for both stepfathers and mothers was associated with agreement between spouses that stepfathers should not assume a parental role quickly, especially the disciplinary component of the role. After two and half years of marriage, however, better marital adjustment in stepfathers was associated with his spending more time in child care, as well as agreement between spouses that he should form a relationship with his stepchildren. After five to seven years of remarriage, such behaviors or beliefs were not associated with marital adjustment for either stepfathers or their spouses."**[6]

Point out to the group that this corresponds with research indicating that better relationships develop between stepparent/stepchild when the stepparent does not assume a major disciplinary role too early.

Stepparents want to be involved in the day-to-day lives of their stepchildren and to influence them for the good. The best approach? Pass out copies of "Tips for Stepparents" (RS-7C). If time allows, have volunteers read them aloud.

Say: **Many stepparents wrongly see their stepchildren as unfinished projects which require their special effort to complete satisfactorily in the few remaining years before they leave home. Effort is given to shaping them up—an effort which meets with anger and resistance in the children, and frustration for the stepparent.**

Pass out two copies of "The Cycle of Anger" (RS-7D) to each participant. One is to be used as a work sheet during this session; the other is to take home and photocopy as needed.

Explain that stepparents may encounter angry feelings when attempting to discipline. This sheet will help them understand what is happening and how their children feel.

To help them understand the sheet, explain the cycle: **When we react to what children do, we are often caught in this parent-child cycle of anger. Remember, this is a cycle, so you can start at any spot in it and it won't change. What we feel impacts what we do. What we do impacts what others think and feel and do. That creates certain thoughts and feelings within, causing us to react ("do") again. And around and around.**

To break the cycle we must find where we are and

*I*t helps clarify the situation if we can determine who has the problem in any given instance.

rather than reacting, respond to the problem in an appropriate manner.

Now select a current discipline problem. Record the child's name. Chart what is happening by filling in some specifics for each point on the cycle, trying to put yourself in the child's shoes for the "child thinks/feels" section. At what point can the cycle be broken? Allow time for reflection.

❻ When Do You Take Action?

Objective:
To help parents determine when it is necessary to modify their child's behavior (10 minutes).

Explain that it isn't always clear when we should jump in and handle a problem with discipline or help a child handle it.

It helps clarify the situation if we can determine who has the problem in any given instance. The person who has a problem because an expectation isn't met is the one who needs to act. For parents, that might mean discipline. For children, it may mean obedience.

Read aloud the following problem situations. Encourage the participants to decide whose problem it is in each case. Then pick one or two situations to discuss in more detail, i.e., how might the problem be solved; should discipline be involved; how to help the child manage, etc.

PROBLEM: Children are talking and laughing loudly in a restaurant. (This is a parent problem. The parents are expecting their children not to disturb others in a public place. Have expectations been communicated ahead of time? Is restaurant appropriate to age of children? What might be appropriate consequences for misbehavior?)

PROBLEM: Your stepchild, while visiting, breaks a curfew always kept by your own children of the same age. (Parents' problem. You expect the child to be home by a certain time. Were expectations specific and clearly communicated? Does your spouse share this expectation and did you discuss it in advance?)

PROBLEM: Your daughter is upset because her stepsister keeps borrowing clothes without permission. (Child's problem. But this has the potential to become a parent problem if the stepparent places blame on the spouse for the child's behavior. You need to keep the problem in perspective and then help the stepsiblings deal with it.)

Be willing to spend time earning respect and the privilege of authority.

PROBLEM: Your child walks at the edge of a busy street. (Parents' problem. Parents should teach children to walk safely. If the child knows better, discipline is needed.)

PROBLEM: Your son says his football coach picks on him. (Child's problem. Children have expectations of their relationships with other adults and must learn to cope. As a parent, it is wise to clarify the situation by checking the facts.)

PROBLEM: Your stepchild doesn't wash the towels as asked. (Parents' problem. Your goal of accomplished chores and clean towels is blocked by the child's actions. If the child doesn't live with you all the time, are you certain he or she knows how to operate the washer and dryer? Have you assigned chores similar to the ones performed at home? Is the distribution of work among biological and stepchildren fair?)

As you close say: **Be willing to spend time earning respect and the privilege of authority. Unless the children believe you have their best interests at heart, you will be swiftly cast into the role of evil stepparent or bully.**

Close the session by having the parents stand, join hands and read the prayer you have written on poster board ahead of time.

> **Father God, You parent us perfectly and love us and our children completely. Please teach us to be the kind of parents and stepparents You want us to be. Help us bring honor to You and peace to our blended families through Jesus Christ. Amen.**

Notes:

1. Emily B. Visher and John S. Visher, *Old Loyalties, New Ties: Therapeutic Strategies with Stepfamilies* (New York: Brunner/Mazel Inc., 1988), p. 19.

2. William Coleman, *What You Should Know About Getting Along With a New Parent* (Minneapolis, Minn.: Augsburg, 1992), p. 11.

3. Visher and Visher, p. 216.

4. Ibid., p. 93.

5. H. Norman Wright, *The Power of a Parent's Words* (Ventura, Calif.:, Regal Books, 1991), p. 45.

6. *Stepfamilies*, Summer, 1993, p. 10.

Wrestling with Time

8

Session Aim:
To equip blended families with effective scheduling and time management tips that reflect Christian priorities.

The problem of scheduling and time management certainly isn't unique to blended families. But, for a couple trying to integrate their families while building and sustaining a new marriage, there are additional tasks to manage and make time for. For their children, time with a parent is vital.

"Time is like oxygen. There is a minimal amount that is needed to survive. Less than that amount may cause permanent damage. And I think the same holds true for a child's time and exposure to both parents," writes Armand Nicoli, a Harvard University psychiatrist.[1]

Individuals in blended families are in transition during the early years especially. They will often feel that most of their world is beyond their control. Time management skills will help them feel that they are progressing toward a definite goal by imparting a sense of purpose.

It is particularly important for couples to seriously look at their priorities. The bottom line of time management is, after all, setting priorities. They will be challenged to ask themselves difficult questions: "What do I consider most important? What (or Who) is the organizing principle of my life? Is my life reflecting these priorities or am I merely saying empty words?"

Acknowledg[ing] the world as it is . . . helps you let go of the notion that somehow things will return to the "good old days."

Getting Ready

Scripture:
Luke 10:38-42; Matthew 4:1-11; Matthew 14:23; Mark 6:30, 31.

1. Prepare copies of "The Tyranny of Choice" (RS-8A), "Priority Pie" (RS-8B), "Stepfamily Tasks" (RS-8C) and also "Evaluating Activities" (RS-8D), if you are having the longer session. Every person should have two copies of "Priority Pie" (RS-8B). Don't forget to three-hole punch if necessary.
2. Following the directions in Step 2, prepare in advance your own copy of "Priority Pie" (RS-8B).
3. If you are doing the longer session, turn to Step 5 where time-saving tips and suggestions are listed. Write each statement in bold type on a slip of paper. Fold these slips of paper in half and put them in a shoe box, coffee can, or hat.
4. You will also need a board or newsprint to write on, Bibles, pens, pencils, and lined paper.

❶ Acknowledge the World As It Is

Objective:
To provide a clear, undeniable portrait of the hectic pace of modern people and to stress the importance of making choices (10 minutes).

Pass out "The Tyranny of Choice" (RS-8A). Read the instructions out loud. Keep the mood light. It's possible that participants will look at the list and say, "I make all these decisions, all the time."

When they are finished, ask them to tally their scores in the box on the bottom of the page. There are twenty-five decisions listed. These are only a few of the possible decisions each of us is called upon to make in a relatively short period.

Ask participants to think of a few other decisions they are continually making. Don't write these down or linger on this exercise too long. Just give them a chance to compare notes.

After a couple of minutes, read these excerpts from Jeff Davidson's book, *Breathing Space*. (Davidson is an award-winning author of books about business and home management.)

"The ability to simply acknowledge the world as it is—no modest task—helps you to let go of the erroneous notion that somehow things will return to the 'good old days.' "[2]

"Before he was twenty-four, your grandfather acquired enough knowledge to make a good living for his whole life. Such a deal is not available to you."[3]

According to Groman's "New Product News," in 1978 a typical supermarket carried 11,767 items. By 1987 that figure more than doubled to 24,531. Hallmark cards offers cards for 105 family relationships.

Think of priorities as portions of a pie, rather than a list of most important to least important.

There are more than 1,000 varieties of shampoo available.[4]

We are going to have to make choices and there's no escaping it. On what are we going to base these choices?

❷ Honest Priorities

Objective:
To help group members evaluate how they are spending time and what this indicates about their priorities (10 minutes).

Give each group member two copies of "Priority Pie" (RS-8B). Ask everyone to write "Reality" across the blank line on one sheet and "My Plan" across the top of the other.

Tell them they will want a separate sheet of paper for making notes or they can use the backs of their resource sheets.

Think of priorities as portions of a pie, rather than a list of most important to least important. With a prioritized "list," the least important are often left undone. While some of these activities may seem less important than, say, prayer or spending time with children, they are still important. Also, some are negotiable (like reading) while others are nonnegotiable (like sleeping).

The unsliced pie represents the entirety of our time. Most important priorities are given larger slices, but less important aren't eliminated, just sliced thinner. On this sheet, you can systematically decide your goals for your blended family, your marriage, and your ministry.

There are various activities listed on the pie chart. These are only suggestions. Using them to get started, ask participants to talk about their priorities as a couple, as well as individually. Suggest they use the sheet labelled "Reality" to determine how they are actually using their time, now.

Some participants might find it helpful to list their daily tasks on a separate sheet of paper with the amount of time dedicated to each activity. They should transfer this information to a visual form by "slicing" the pie into time slices set aside for each activity. You should have done this in advance yourself (see Getting Ready, #2). This will provide a sample they can view to help understand what's expected.

When they have roughed out the "Reality" of how they're currently spending time, they may work on "My Plan" to give more time to activities that should have more priority. This will be a working plan for better time management. Most of the group members will not have time to complete it, but you will be returning to it later.

Priorities determine choices. Choices take up my time.

After giving them seven or eight minutes to work on the two sheets, ask them to set it aside for now. On the board or newsprint write, **"Priorities determine choices. Choices take up my time."**

Then say: **When we become aware and intentional about our priorities, choices reflect those priorities. So, priorities give us a basis for making choices. Choices are the natural result of priorities the same way water is the natural issue of rain clouds.**

❸ Choosing the Good or the Better

Objective:
To give group members a biblical understanding of what is most important (10-15 minutes).

Reaching a good balance between time with others, time for accomplishing various tasks, and time alone is no easy matter. So, we turn to the Bible to learn why and how.

Ask a volunteer to read Luke 10:38-42, the story of Mary and Martha. Then ask: **What was Martha's priority? How did that priority determine her choice?** (Her priority was being a good hostess and making her guests comfortable. She chose her tasks over being with her guest. She chose doing something for Jesus, rather than being with Jesus.)

What was Mary's priority? How did that priority determine her choice? (Her priority was being with Jesus, listening to Him. She chose this over tasks and chores.)

Are either of their choices bad? (It is a good thing to serve and prepare. It is a good thing to be with Jesus. The choice is between a good activity and a better one.)

What are some of your own experiences with choices between good activities and better ones? (Answers might include such things as resting on Sunday morning or going to worship services. Shopping for your new coat or playing softball with your child, etc.)

Many of us feel guilty when we slow down and don't try to do it all. When Martha scurried about serving her guests, this was a good thing. Yet Jesus told her it's better to sit still and listen to Him. There's no reason to feel guilty when you have chosen the better way.

Jesus did not let the pressures of the urgent stop Him from keeping the most important things most important. He withdrew frequently into solitude and silence. His ministry was launched after forty days alone

(Matt. 4:1-11). **After feeding five thousand He headed for solitude** (Matt. 14:23).

He also instructed His disciples to do the same. **After they returned from ministering, He told them, "Come with me by yourselves to a quiet place and get some rest"** (Mark 6:31).

Write the three Scripture references mentioned above on the board as you talk. Then ask: **How can you carve out time for what is most important and for solitude?**

There are no right and wrong answers in this discussion. If the group bogs down in discussion about solitude, read this excerpt and ask for their reactions:

In his book, *A Center of Quiet,* **David Runcorn writes, "So many things in life possess us and claim us for themselves. And in our turn we claim and possess others . . . solitude and silence are places where all that can be untangled. We are given back to ourselves to start again."**[5]

Read this excerpt by Charlie Shedd:

"We assign ourselves an overload, but never the Lord. He knows what He wants from each of us, and there is plenty of time in His day for things essential to His plan. We do Him a grave injustice when we fall into the habit of compulsive overwork. We sin when we pressure out His wishes for assignments that have not been filtered through divine judgment. Self-centered scheduling that wants it our way and ours alone, is far different from setting up a plan with the [Holy Spirit] as our guide."[6]

❹ Setting Your Goals

Objective:
The group members will set goals for themselves and their blended families (10-15 minutes).

There is an old saying, "The one who aims at nothing is certain to hit it." Along the same lines, the one who aims at too many targets will rarely hit all of them. How can goals help us accomplish our priorities?

A short discussion should bring out these points:
(Goal setting . . .
1. Establishes a direction and narrows our focus.
2. Provides a guideline for making choices. If some activity does not support a goal, we know that activity is probably not important.
3. Gives us a reasonable understanding of our limits.)

It is important to keep the number of life goals manageable. Six or seven goals for our lives are plenty.

Ask the group to brainstorm what might be important goals for Christians in blended families. Write these on the board, but encourage the group members to write them down and use them while they are setting their own goals.

It is important to keep the number of life goals manageable. Six or seven goals for our lives are plenty. We will establish subgoals to reinforce these, but the focus we determine should be fairly narrow.

When the list goes over five goals, ask the group if any are subgoals (for example, "Read the Bible more" is a subgoal of "Grow spiritually"), or whether any goal is more important than the ones on the list already. Don't let this exercise go on for too long.

The list might look something like this:
(1. Grow closer to God and mature spiritually.
2. Strengthen my marriage.
3. Be a better parent and stepparent.
4. Serve others with the gifts God has given me.
5. Develop strong friendships.
6. Stay healthy.
7. Discover creative and pleasurable work.)

Notice that almost any subgoal will fit one of these goals for Christians. A life goals list should be broad; it might help the participants to think of it as a mission statement.

Give couples time now to work on their pie charts again. Suggest they write out a mission statement together if they are having trouble coming up with goals.

Read this example of a mission statement by Tony Campolo: **"Before I hang up my sneakers at the end, I want to have motivated and helped at least two hundred college and university students to commit themselves to go out as full-time missionaries for the cause of Christ."**[7]

This is a very specific mission statement. Suggest couples write something similar reflecting their goal for their blended family.

Pass out copies of "Stepfamily Tasks" (RS-8C), explaining that this is informational only. Also distribute "Evaluating Activities" (RS-8D), and encourage participants to use these questions to help them evaluate requests on their time.

*T*he problem of scheduling and time management certainly isn't unique to blended families.

❺ Getting in Focus

Objective:

To help couples focus their few main goals and begin developing supporting short term goals for these (5-10 minutes).

Refer the group back to the basic goals in Step 4. Pick one or two of these to discuss. Write one on the board, for example: "Be a better stepparent."

This is the stated goal. What can you do this week or soon that will help you accomplish this? Ask participants to brainstorm a few subgoals. For example, "better stepparent" subgoals might include:

(• Have lunch with my stepchild once a week
• Read a book about stepparenting
• Pray for my stepchild daily
• Ask my stepchild about his or her feelings
• Help my spouse understand how I feel about this child)

Walk through this process for two main goals. If you have additional time, have the group break into small groups of two couples, or four persons, to discuss their goals, helping one another develop subgoals. Encourage couples to continue this process at home, developing goals and steps to meet those goals.

Bring the group back together and close the session with prayer, asking for wisdom and insight as we plan lives that will bring honor to the kingdom of God.

Notes:

1. Armand Nicoli, "The Real Issue" newsletter, April, 1992, p. 13.
2. Jeff Davidson, *Breathing Space* (New York: Master Media, 1991), p. 16.
3. Ibid, p. 23.
4. Ibid, p. 27.
5. David Runcorn, *A Center of Quiet* (Downers Grove, Ill.: InterVarsity Press, 1990), p. 54.
6. Charlie Shedd, quoted by Ted Engstrom in *Redeeming Time* (Wheaton, Ill.: Harold Shaw, 1991), p. 13.
7. Tony Campolo, *Everything You've Heard Is Wrong* (Dallas, Tex.: Word, 1992), p. 118.

So Much Family, So Little Time

9

There is an old African proverb that goes, "It takes a village to raise a child." As divorce and other cultural influences force us to look seriously at our ideas of what a family is, all of us will be confronted with the importance of community.

Stepfamilies must handle the challenge of new and changing family images every day. Divorce emphasizes two separate sides of the child's family—Mom's side and Dad's side. Then remarriage introduces an entirely new complication. Children may also have their stepfather's family and their stepmother's family.

The numbers of relationships can make parents feel as if they are indeed raising their children and conducting their lives in a small village of relatives.

This situation presents some problems. Some problems involve personal relationships that are new or broken. Some of the problems concern having time to stay connected with more family than the new couple may have anticipated.

In the last half of this century mobility and job transfers have dispersed relatives all across the country to the point that living in and experiencing extended family is foreign to many modern Americans. In this session, we'll consider the important role extended family and community plays in the health of blended families.

There is an old African proverb that goes, "It takes a village to raise a child."

Getting Ready

Scripture:
John 3:1; Romans 8:15-17;
John 1:12, 13; II Corinthians
6:18; Luke 2:48-52; 8:19-21;
I John 3:13-15; 3:16-18.

1. Poster and art supplies you'll need for the project in Step 1 include: name tag and poster board or large newsprint for each person; an assortment of old magazines and used greeting cards; colored markers, crayons, and pencils; scissors, glue, rulers, and tape.
2. In advance, write this list of possible relatives on the board or newsprint: grandparents, stepgrandparents, father, mother, stepparents, siblings, stepsiblings, aunts, uncles, cousins, steprelatives on stepmother's side, steprelatives on stepfather's side.
3. Participants will need a surface to draw or paste on. Large, long tables are best. Plan for this in advance.
4. Prepare copies of "Extending the Borders of Family" (RS-9A), and "Bridging the Gaps" (RS-9B). If needed, three-hole punch.
5. Also have extra index cards, lined paper, Bibles, and pens.
6. If using Step 5, write the two statements on page 65 on newsprint or the board ahead of time.

❶ Getting It Clear

Objective:
To have parents create a family portrait from the perspective of one of their children (10 minutes).

As parents arrive, give them each a large sheet of newsprint or poster board and have them print the words "Family Portrait" in large letters across the top. Hand out name tags; tell them to put the name of one of their children on the name tag and take on that child's identity for the next 10 minutes.

They will draw a portrait or cut out pictures from magazines to compile a family portrait including all old and new family members. Suggest they use the list on the board to keep them from forgetting any family members. Have a place to hang the posters.

❷ Family Ties That Bind

Objective:
To help couples sort through the problems and joys associated with having so much family (10 minutes).

Begin by asking how they felt when they were thinking like a child about the complicated family structure. Let one or two people talk briefly before going on. (They will probably say things such as: confused, overwhelmed, frustrated, disconnected, etc.)

Extended family is a very complicated matter in blended families. This isn't news to those who have finished trying to chart their family group. Say: **There are benefits to both the children and couples in extended families.**

On the board or a sheet of newsprint make two columns

There are benefits to both the children and couples in extended families.

labeled **DRAWBACKS** and **BENEFITS**.

First discuss the drawbacks of having so many relatives to consider. As they are mentioned, write them in the DRAWBACKS column. Then do the same with the benefits. Whenever possible, turn a negative into a positive.

Drawbacks that might be mentioned:
(There's not enough time for everyone.
Resentment toward relatives, broken relationships.
Disagreement over spiritual matters.
Relatives interfere.
Relatives are demanding.
Children don't feel close to relatives.
Relatives bring up bad memories.
They complicate holidays, birthdays, etc.)

Benefits that might be mentioned:
(Family can help support during hard times.
Older family members have a wealth of experience to draw on.
Family gives children a sense of belonging.
Family validates the reality and importance of their heritage.
There are more persons who care about you.
Community is a gift of God to help us grow as persons.
Family can give a couple a break from child-rearing tasks to have more time together.
Family adds enjoyment to holidays.
Family loves you in spite of your mistakes.
Family reinforces certain values—respect for elders, sharing, loyalty.
Good preparation for becoming an in-law.
Continued family relationships reduces disruption to children's lives.
New family contacts helps children learn how to build relationships.)

Be careful the discussion doesn't turn into a gripe session. An honest discussion of extended family must include the negatives, but don't get stuck or linger there too long. Strive to have the positives outweigh the negatives.

Be sure to end this section with a positive result of community. **Perhaps the most important benefit to us and our children is that through relating to our families, God**

But you cannot become human on your own . . . the one thing a clenched fist cannot do is accept."

will grow us up into people who more closely resemble what God had in mind when He made people. This is the purpose of all community, including family.

Christian novelist Frederick Buechner writes, "The trouble with steeling yourself against the harshness of reality is that the same steel that secures your life against being destroyed secures your life also against being opened up and transformed by the holy power that life itself comes from. You can survive on your own. You can grow strong on your own. You can even prevail on your own. But you cannot become human on your own . . . the one thing a clenched fist cannot do is accept."[1]

Suggest that the group prayerfully consider, during a moment of silence, whether or not they have been willing to accept the gift and action of God through their extended families. Move on after a minute or so.

❸ The Borders of Family

Objective:
To give couples in a blended family a biblical understanding of how community and extended family parallels God's redemptive adoption of humankind (15 minutes).

Pass out "Extending the Borders of Family" (RS-9A). Read the top few lines aloud:

The Fatherhood of God beckons all people into a family relationship with one another. Blended families model this reality because some of our ties are biological and some aren't. Read the passages and answer the questions in each section.

Give participants seven or eight minutes to complete the resource sheet. If you wish, you may divide them into small groups for this section.

Call the group together and ask if they have any comments or questions about the resource sheet. Then discuss the questions in each section. Draw out the following points in your discussion:

• Benefits of a spiritual rebirth include:

I John 3:1—(As children of God we will experience God's love and receive His Spirit.)

Romans 8:15-17—(We can call God "Daddy" and "Father.")

John 1:12, 13—(We become children of God.)

II Corinthians 6:18—(We become the Lord's sons and daughters.)

The Fatherhood of God beckons all people into a family relationship with one another.

• Jesus' definition of His family included:
Luke 2:48-52—(God the Father)
Luke 8:19-21—(Those who hear God's Word and put it into practice)

• Traits of our spiritual extended family we can model in our own blended families include:
I John 3:13-15—(Love)
I John 3:16, 17—(Sacrifice)
I John 3:18—(Love in action, not only words)

Stress the importance of two concepts here: Love and self-sacrifice (or unselfishness).

❹ On the Homefront

Objective:
To give group members practical, loving, unselfish ways of managing their network of relatives (10 minutes).
NOTE: If time is short, this will be your last section. End with the prayer suggestion on page 65.

Pass out "Bridging the Gaps" (RS-9B). Tell the group that together you will try to help each other work through some of the problems faced in stepfamily relations.

In this discussion stress that group members should apply the principles learned in the earlier section: love and self-sacrifice. Whenever possible, offer any suggestions following the discussion topic. Encourage participants to share what is working for them, and to take notes on their resource sheet of what works for others. The best information will be passed on this way.

1. Adults and children spending time with relatives on holidays, birthdays, special events.
(Flexibility is important here. Try to establish a tradition early in your blended family relationships and stick with it. If changes are necessary, plan ahead as much as possible.)

2. Staying in touch with a former spouse's family so that the children retain a strong sense of connection to where they came from.
(Help the child build his or her own family photo album and history by turning over whatever family mementos you have from your former spouse's family.)

(Encourage the child to stay in touch with someone in the family who can pass on news of births, anniversaries, reunions, etc. This is especially important if the child's other parent isn't close to his or her family.)

(Encourage all family members to write family histories to be included in your family records.)

3. Guarding time for your blended family.

(Schedule time together and stick to your plans. Together plan activities everyone will enjoy.

(Be sure the children understand your expectation that they will participate and how they will participate.

(Be willing to work around the schedules of family members. This is really important with junior and senior high age children.)

4. Encouraging extended family relationships, for example those between cousins of close ages or grandparents.

(Letters, phone calls, post cards, videos, and tape recordings help people stay in touch. Cousins can visit your house during summer vacation. Perhaps the children can spend an occasional weekend with grandparents. Keep grandparents informed about special activities.)

5. Developing new family ties with steprelatives.

(Honor the children by following their lead in this; don't force them into relationships. At the same time, encourage them to stretch their relating abilities by giving new family members a chance to become part of their lives.

(Be patient with new steprelatives. Some will be able to accept new family members easier than others. It is important that no one be forced into closeness.)

Leave a few minutes for participants to think over and respond to the question at the bottom of the resource sheet. Offer extra paper if anyone needs it.

❺ Belonging in the Greatest Sense

Objective:
To encourage participants to develop supportive relationships within the local church, who can also be extended family for them (15 minutes).

According to the experts, "belonging" can be a major issue within stepfamilies. There are divisions built into the arrangement at first. "Turf" is a major issue with stepfamilies. Insiders and outsiders can quickly form within a household unless an effort is made to counter this tendency. One set of grandparents, perhaps not the biological ones, becomes the favorite of the parents for Sunday visits and the others become grandparents of the past, the outsiders.[2]

People naturally feel more attached to those who are more familiar to them, or more similar to themselves.

At times of tension, households naturally divide

At times of tension, households naturally divide along biological lines.

along biological lines.[3] There need to be shifts in these alignments, but these come slowly.

In the Bible study section, we discussed how extended family is similar to the family of God or Christian community in that God looks beyond the nuclear family. Here are two more parallels. Can you think of others?

Write these on newsprint or the board ahead of time:
- **Those not biologically related become family.**
- **We experience a sense of belonging rather than being an outsider.**

After five minutes of discussion, ask the couples to think about how the extended "family of God" or the church has been their family, or has supported them. Allow plenty of time for group sharing.

Use their discussion to remind them that they can be family for each other too. Give each couple an index card. Ask them to write their names, phone number, and family prayer requests that they are willing to share with other group members. Collect these and redistribute them to the group, being sure every couple has the name and phone number of another couple.

During the week pray for the family on your card and call them at least once to tell them of your concern. Be alert to any other ways God might enable you to support them.

Have the group join hands and spend a few minutes praying either silently or aloud for one another. Close by praying aloud that each group member will become increasingly aware of belonging to the family of God. If your group includes unbelievers, pray they will become more and more aware of God's love and His desire to have them in His family.

NOTE: If you are going to distribute catalogs from local Christian bookstores or mail order houses during Session 11 (see page 74), collect them this week.

Notes:

1. Frederick Buechner, *Sacred Journey* (New York: Harper San Francisco, 1982), p. 46.
2. Emily B. Visher and John S. Visher, *Old Loyalties, New Ties* (New York: Brunner/Mazel, 1988), summarized from chapter six.
3. Ibid, p. 138.

Building Blocks of Trust

10

Session Aim:
To give blended families practical help in the process of building trust in their family relationships.

As noted before, blended families are families birthed in loss. Because of the serious loss these people have experienced, many will be reluctant to trust. Many will have problems entering new relationships or believing that the future can be any better than their wounded past. It's a struggle for adults and children alike.

The struggle is twofold: demonstrating one's trustworthiness to others, and believing in the commitments others say they have made to us.

Moving forward as a family means dealing head-on with issues of trust and commitment. When we've been hurt, our natural inclination is to build self-protective walls to keep others out.

Dr. Donald Joy, professor of Human Development at Asbury Seminary, writes, "The perfect vision of perfect love in human relationships is a dream worth pursuing. Whether most of us achieve it at the level we want is less important than that it hang out there as God's target toward which we aspire."[1]

Joy writes that his favorite "two-line theology" for those who have lived through broken relationships is:

God, who has created all things good,
Can make all things new, through Jesus![2]

God, who has created all things good, can make all things new, through Jesus!"

Getting Ready

Scriptures:
I Corinthians 1:9, 15:58;
Philippians 1:6, Hebrews
10:23, 13:20

1. Make copies of "A Place Where Trust Can Grow" (RS-10A), "Stepfamily Stages" (RS-10B), and "Becoming a Bridge-Builder" (RS-10C).
2. For Step 2, prepare six index cards ahead of time, writing one of the six "qualities" on each card (see page 68). When participants arrive, give the index cards to six "volunteers" who will each read one quality aloud at the appropriate time.
3. You will need newsprint or a board to write on and extra paper, Bibles, and pens or pencils.

❶ Experiencing Trust

Objective:
Group members will briefly explore their individual experiences in trusting relationships (5 minutes).

Because blended families have histories of broken relationships, and broken promises, the very thing blended families need most to make them whole is what is sometimes the hardest to give—trust.

All of us have had experience with trusting and having that trust violated. But we have usually had people in our lives who have also been trustworthy.

Ask participants to think of someone in whom they trust; it should be someone other than their spouse or God.

What is it that person has done or continues to do that reinforces his or her trust? How has this person demonstrated trustworthiness?

Participants will probably name their parents, grandparents, brother or sister, best friend, teacher, or pastor along with others. Be prepared to write down in one or two words the traits or actions of those people they trust.

Guide the group to this understanding of their trusting relationships:

• **Trust happens in the circle of relationships; it is a dynamic of loving, long-term relationships.**

• **These are positive relationships in which persons feel affirmed and encouraged.**

• **The relationships endure through good and bad times.**

• **When under fire, the trusted person has shown himself or herself trustworthy.**

• **The trustworthy person is committed to us.**

Then share the following:

Trust is a key element in lasting relationships. However, it does not just happen. It is not something auto-

matic in a relationship. Even if we extend to others a degree of trust early in relationships, that trust is withdrawn easily and quickly.

According to stepfamily researchers and therapists Emily and John Visher, trust in stepfamilies is "tentative at best" in the early stages of integration.[3]

The fledgling relationships need time and experience such as those we've known in our trusting relationships.

One of the most important things stepparents can do is nurture and create a home environment where trust can grow naturally.

❷ A Place Where Trust Can Grow

Objective:
Give couples information they can use in how to create a trusting environment in their homes (15 minutes).

Stepfamilies are healing families. According to an article in *Christian Parenting Today*,[4] families who enable healing demonstrate these six qualities:

These qualities will be written out in advance on index cards and distributed to volunteers to read. Ask the volunteers to rise according to the number in the corner of the cards they are reading. Suggest that other group members write them down as they are read.

1. Families who heal work at unconditional acceptance.
2. Families who heal set consistent rules and expectations.
3. Families who heal respect privacy and individual worth.
4. Families who heal are not devastated by conflict. Instead, they develop methods to deal with it.
5. In families who heal, people listen to each other.
6. Families who heal don't gloss over mistakes and hurts, but work to forgive and resolve.

After going through these traits, pass out copies of "A Place Where Trust Can Grow" (RS-10A). **If trust is going to grow, we must become families who heal. Just as we can help nurture a safe, loving environment in our homes, we can do the opposite with some attitudes.**

Divide participants into two or three small groups and ask them to work on the resource sheet in their groups. Explain that they should talk briefly about why the stated attitude can damage rather than build trust. They should then write down the opposite, positive, or healing attitude in the blank box.

A major factor in building relationships and building trust is TIME.

When they have finished, bring the group back together for a brief discussion. Don't stress right and wrong answers, but here are some possible responses.

1. My perspective is the right one. (I will accept your viewpoint.)
2. Be logical. (Feelings are acceptable.)
3. Follow the rules. (Let's talk about the rules.)
4. Be practical. (Tell me about your dreams.)
5. Avoid ambiguity. (I don't have to understand every thing.)
6. To err is wrong. (Everyone makes mistakes.)
7. Play is a waste of time. (Play is a gift of God.)
8. I don't do it that way. (I want to learn new ways.)
9. Don't be foolish. (I'll listen to your ideas.)
10. I'm not the creative sort. (I'm willing to give this a chance.)

It's important to remember that stepfamilies need time to grow together as a family. In everything we've talked about, we've discussed how important it is to establish trust in relationships. Remember that a major factor in building relationships and building trust is TIME.

Stepfamilies, according to experts, can expect definable stages of family integration. Some say there are seven steps, and some suggest eight phases.

Pass out "Stepfamily Stages" (RS-10B). Explain that this information will help couples locate where they are in the integration process. This will help them understand what trust-building tasks are yet to be accomplished.

Suggest that couples take time to go over this sheet later, together, and talk about where they are in the stages.

Say: **It is possible for one person to be a step behind the other. This is nothing to be concerned about as long as the couple continues talking to each other.**

The bedrock beneath trust, holding it up, is commitment, an act of our will.

❸ Commitment: The Foundation of Relationships

Objective:
To provide couples with information about the implications of commitment (10 minutes).
NOTE: If you are doing the shorter session, go to step 4.

Trust springs from lasting, committed relationships. The bedrock beneath trust, holding it up, is commitment, an act of our will. Commitment sustains trust, it gives us the courage to risk ourselves with others.

According to Jon Johnston, the author of *Walls or Bridges: How to Build Relationships that Glorify God,* **relationships require total commitment.**[5]

Write the following commitments (shown in bold) on the board or on newsprint. Do not record the answer in parentheses on the board.

Ask group participants what part of themselves is involved in making each commitment. Keep the discussion focused as suggested below, stressing complete commitment to one another. Also, emphasize that any commitment requires a decision, an act of the will. We can't just slide into a commitment, or it won't last.

Commitment to risk (emotions)
Commitment of time and involvement (physical)
Commitment to build and not tear down (lips and mind)
Commitment to endurance (spiritual)

It might be helpful to mention that this is the same kind of commitment God makes to us and we make to Him.

❹ The Founder of Faithfulness

Objective:
To help diminish couples' fear of commitment because of God's faithfulness to believers (10-15 minutes).

Divide participants into small groups for a short Bible study and say: **The ultimate model for us to follow in trustworthiness is God. God is completely faithful to us. We can also depend on God to help us be trustworthy and faithful.**

Write the following five Scripture passages on the board or newsprint. You may assign all of them to each group, or you may decide to divide them between groups if you have less time to work with.

Give group members time to study the passage(s) together, concentrating on what each tells us about God's faithfulness.

After a few minutes, bring the group back together and discuss what they discovered.

• **I Corinthians 15:58**—(Do not be moved, remember that what you do is not in vain in the Lord.)

"Those of us who claim to be twice-born, must understand the dynamics of godly relationships."

- **Philippians 1:6**—(God has begun a good work in us and our families. God is faithful and we can count on His faithfulness to finish the work.)
- **I Corinthians 1:9**—(God has called us and demonstrated His faithfulness. We can rest on God's dependability.)
- **Hebrews 10:23**—(We have reason to hold without doubt to God. God is completely trustworthy.)
- **Hebrews 13:20, 21**—(God, whom we know is faithful, is also the equipper. We don't need to rely on our own abilities, but can trust God to provide us with whatever a situation calls for.)

After the Bible study ask participants these questions to stimulate discussion:

If you have experienced that God is trustworthy, how has that happened?

As you grow in your relationship with God, is it harder or easier for you to trust God? Why?

What can we learn from God about encouraging others to trust us?

❺ A Home without Walls

Objective:
To help couples apply what they have learned to their own home situation (10 minutes).

"Those of us who claim to be twice-born, must understand the dynamics of godly relationships. Then, with God's guidance and power, we must demolish unsightly walls in order to construct bridges to other people, regardless of our temperament," writes Christian author Jon Johnston in *Walls or Bridges: How to Build Relationships that Glorify God.*[6]

Sometimes it is our temperament and our usual way of doing things, or our usual way of thinking, that creates walls between us and other people. To help us escape these ways of relating to others, we must consider our contribution to wall building.

Pass out "Becoming a Bridge-Builder" (RS-10C). Go over the content with the group, allowing for a few minutes of discussion about the difference between building walls and building bridges.

Wrap up the discussion by inviting participants to spend a few minutes in private reflection with the resource sheet. Suggest they put their chairs a little ways apart for the sake of internal reflection. **In what ways or areas are you building**

walls? building bridges? Suggest that they write down their thoughts.

❻ Stepping toward Trust

Objective:
To provide suggestions for practical ways couples can build trust in their families (5 minutes).

Bring the group back together in a tight circle and announce that you'll have a brainstorming session for practical ways to build trust in their families. Ask couples to share what has worked in their families.

Participants might share ideas such as the following:

(• Be present at activities, sports events, performances, etc.
• Keep your promises.
• Establish dependable routines in the ordinary tasks of driving children to school, giving lunch money and allowances, providing boundaries, etc.
• Take secrets and confidentiality seriously.
• Honor privacy.
• Remember birthdays and other special times.
• Be creative in showing your affection and interest.)

End the session by praying that God will help each couple grow in trust for the other members of their family and also in their own faithfulness to the family.

Notes:

1. Donald Joy, *Rebonding: Preventing and Restoring Damaged Relationships* (Waco, Tex.: Word, 1986), p. 81.
2. Ibid.
3. Emily B. Visher and John S. Visher, *Old Loyalties, New Ties* (New York: Brunner/Mazel, 1988), p. 191.
4. Timothy Boyd, "Families Who Heal," *Christian Parenting Today*, January/February 1991, pp. 47-52.
5. Jon Johnston, *Walls or Bridges: How to Build Relationships that Glorify God* (Grand Rapids, Mich.: Baker, 1988), pp. 56-68.
6. Ibid., p. 14.

Shaping Family 11 Spirituality

Session Aim:
To help parents in blended families set goals for family spiritual formation and discover resources to reach those goals.

As in any Christian family, remarried couples are concerned about the spiritual development of their children. Ideally, this is initiated, sustained, and nurtured in the family setting.

Family spirituality presents a special challenge to a stepfamily. Persons have been brought together who have a spiritual history. It is possible that children were given some spiritual guidance in their parent's previous marriage. Any discussion of blended family spirituality must deal realistically with the past each person brings to the newly forming family.

It is important to stress individual spiritual development, especially for parents, as a means of encouraging children in spiritual matters. All members of the family must be treated with respect. Coercion or force will only lead to rebellion.

In this session, couples will be challenged to follow a course of spiritual growth while gently leading their fledgling families along the same path.

God has ordained the disciplines of the spiritual life as the means by which we place ourselves where he can bless us."

Getting Ready

Scripture:
II Corinthians 4:7; 7:1; 10:3-5.

1. Make enough copies of "The Spiritual Disciplines: A Primer" (RS-11A), "Spiritual Development of Children" (RS-11B), and "A Spiritual Plan" (RS-11C) for everyone.
2. You will need Bibles, lined paper, pens, newsprint or board to write on.
3. Participants will need a writing surface if you don't have tables for them.
4. Gather catalogs from Christian bookstores, publishers, and mail-order houses. Be sure to have enough for each family.
5. If possible, have a copy of Richard Foster's *Celebration of Discipline* to refer to during the study session. Your pastor or church library might have one.

❶ A Foundational Understanding

Objective:
To identify and emphasize the importance of key spiritual disciplines to the parents' individual and family spirituality (15-20 minutes).

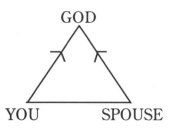

Start by mentioning the importance of a horizontal focus in developing unity in our relationships. Liken human relationships to a triangle. Use marriage as a relationship when drawing attention to this principle. Illustrate by drawing a triangle on the board.

Label the top point with the word, "God." At the two bottom points write the words "You" and "Spouse."

Move your marker or chalk upwards along the side of the triangle.

The closer we get to God, the closer we come to one another. Our moving toward God cuts down the distance between us and others. This is also true in our families.

An important way we move closer to God is through the spiritual disciplines. Richard Foster, in his classic book *Celebration of Discipline*, writes, "By themselves the spiritual disciplines can do nothing; they can only get us to the place where something can be done. They are God's means of grace . . . God has ordained the disciplines of the spiritual life as the means by which we place ourselves where he can bless us."[1]

Why worry about the disciplines when we are "saved by grace?" Because we have been given the gift of salvation, or justification, in "jars of clay" as it says in II Corinthians 4:7.

Ask someone to read II Corinthians 4:7. Then divide the group into smaller groups for a short Bible study and study on the spiritual disciplines.

Pass out a copy of "The Spiritual Disciplines: A Primer" (RS-11A) to each group member. Instruct the group to spend their first few minutes reviewing the top part of the resource sheet. They should write a few words after each spiritual discipline to describe it.

Then call their attention to the question and Scriptures at the bottom of the page. After reading the passages, they should discuss the question and formulate a one paragraph response. Be sure to emphasize, first, review and understand the spiritual disciplines, then do the Bible study.

Give them about five minutes for this task. If you notice they are getting stuck on the spiritual disciplines, suggest they move on to the Bible study.

Begin the discussion by asking them to read their one paragraph responses to the question. If the summaries don't include these points, make an effort to mention them:

(1. Spiritual disciplines are how we are involved in the process of purifying ourselves.)

(2. Spiritual disciplines are our divine weapons, filled with divine power to "demolish strongholds . . . arguments . . . pretensions." II Cor. 10:4, 5)

As a group, review the spiritual disciplines, giving them a chance to discuss them. After each discipline are points you will want to make.

Inward Disciplines

Meditation: Meditation means reflecting, ruminating, rehearsing, listening. By it we hear and obey God. It is learning to practice the presence of God in our ordinary lives.

Prayer: To pray is to seek help, it is the avenue God uses to change us. C. S. Lewis said, "God is not changed by prayer, I am."

Fasting: Fasting is not commanded, but when Jesus speaks of fasting, He assumes it is something believers will do. Primarily, fasting points out the things that control us and teaches us that we are God-sustained.

Study: Study helps us think about God and our human experience. With concentration and purpose, we direct our minds to consider a certain focus. Meditation is devotional, study is intellectual. Repetition, concentration, comprehension and reflection are all part of study. We study the Word of God and writings related to it.

Outward Disciplines

Simplicity: Simplicity liberates us to follow after what matters most. It frees us from cultural norms and moves us into solidarity with the oppressed. It does not mean going without, but accepting and living joyfully with enough. It means sharing.

Solitude (and silence): It centers us on God, breaks down the walls of noise and activity we build between ourselves and God, and ourselves and one another. It frees us from obsession with ourselves.

Submission: In submission we are "released to drop the matter, to forget it." We become more Christ-like as we yield ourselves to others. We are free to stop protecting self-interests and give way to others.

Service: Everyone in the kingdom has equal authority and status. By serving others, we identify with the work of redemption, voluntarily laying down our lives, initiated in Jesus Christ.

Corporate Disciplines

Confession: Confession means honest relationships in which we are free to acknowledge our mistakes and doubts. It makes the forgiveness of God real to us as forgiveness is extended to us by the one to whom we confess.

Worship: To worship in community is to give our whole person over to experiencing, reflecting, and relishing in the reality of God among us.

Guidance: Acknowledges the corporate nature of God's direction and will. It reflects the discipline of submission, a willingness to lay down individual objectives in order to be led together.

Celebration: Corporate celebration reflects the coming of the Year of Jubilee in Jesus Christ and our deliverance from death and sin. It encourages noise, dance, and joyful expressions of God among us.

As spiritual leaders, parents must be honest about their own weaknesses and strengths.

❷ Evaluate Your Own Spirituality

Objective:
To encourage group members to briefly and honestly assess their own spiritual development (5 minutes).

Ask participants to spend a few minutes looking over the list of disciplines and reflecting on their own experiences. Have them answer the question on RS-11A: What disciplines are already part of their experience? In what disciplines do they need to grow? Are there any they don't understand?

They should make personal notes during this process. Stress that as spiritual leaders, parents must be honest about their own weaknesses and strengths.

❸ Childhood Needs

Objective:
To help parents understand the spiritual needs of children at various stages of development (10 minutes).

Bring the group together into a close discussion circle. Pass out "Spiritual Development of Children" (RS-11B). Be sure you have a copy of it also. One by one go through each developmental stage.

Encourage parents to add their own insights. As you review the needs and traits of each stage, ask the group this question: **What kind of family devotions or activities might work best for this age group?** Encourage creativity.

Whenever possible, guide participants into suggestions using these activities and resources:

Skits	Outdoors activities
Writing	Fiction
Using imagination	Reading out loud
Discussion	Storytelling
Drawing and painting	Roleplaying
Videos and music	

❹ Family Spirituality Ideas

Objective:
To brainstorm and discuss ideas for activities that develop family spirituality (10-15 minutes).

If you keep the group in the circle, pass out writing supplies and books or something hard to write on. If possible, move to a table or desks. Be sure everyone has something to write on and with. Keep couples together.

Tell them the group is going to work together on developing ideas for activities that will help their families grow spiritually. You will say a word or phrase aloud. That word is their springboard for discussion. Suggestions and discussion starters follow each word below.

Meals: start with a psalm; serious discussions; conclude with a prayer time.

Calendar: can be used to remember prayer requests; schedule family prayer times; celebrate holy days.

Resource Center: build a library of books, cassettes, CDs, videos; get suggestions for books.

Atmosphere: talk openly about God; play Christian music; have Christian books and magazines sitting around; invite Christian friends to meals; display pictures or plaques with spiritual truth on them.

Devotions: develop as a couple first; consider age of children; pick a format; be creative.

Conversations: ask children questions about where they are spiritually; engage them in conversations about things that matter; talk openly about your faith.

Prayer Place: designate a special chair as a prayer place; turn a spare room into a place for solitude; every time the family is all at the table, begin with prayer; link prayer with places in your house.

Events: Christian concerts; family camp; seminars.

Crisis: there is no shortage of crises in blended families! Times of crisis are good times to let children see you pray and to ask them to pray.

Serving together: serve at a soup kitchen; sing in a nursing home; visit a shut-in. This affirms the gifts of individuals and unites the family in purpose.

Worship: attend church together; be willing to let teenagers attend a church of their choice; worship at home.

Missions: support a missionary as a family; work on a project for a missionary family; pray for different countries daily.

Bibles: have open Bibles in the house; read from Scripture together; have a family Bible study; put a Bible on everyone's bed at night open to a psalm assigned from a lectionary or devotional guide; get specialty Bibles for various age groups.

Trips: pray before trips; find a church to attend when you're on vacation; visit cathedrals, monasteries, retreat centers; memorize a psalm in the car.

Planning: develop a family plan for spirituality; set spiritual goals; use a simple prayer book or liturgical calendar. Planning encourages family members to know what to expect and to plan ahead.

Ask God to guide and support group members as they creatively follow the Lord and help their families do the same.

❺ Write a Plan

Objective:
To have group members set goals and make plans for their families and themselves (5-10 minutes)

In the shorter session, you will only be able to get participants started in their goal-setting. In the longer session, participants should work on developing plans for both their family and as individuals.

Pass out "A Spiritual Plan" (RS-11C). This sheet lists some concrete ideas for developing a family spirituality. These are just to get participants thinking about what they can do to get started.

Group members should break into couples (or pairs) to look over this sheet and talk about their goals. Give them plenty of time to work on this. If you have acquired catalogs from an area Christian book store or a mail-order house, pass these out at this time.

Bring the group into a circle of prayer at the end. Give them a chance to offer thanks for what God is doing in their families. Also ask for prayer requests.

Either assign individuals to pray for various requests or do so yourself. Then close in prayer by asking God to guide and support group members as they creatively and obediently follow the Lord and help their families do the same.

Notes:

1. Richard Foster, *Celebration of Discipline* (San Francisco: Harper & Row, 1978, 1988), p. 7.

Fun, Humor, and Family Nights

12

Session Aim:
To give blended families practical, fun, doable ideas for family activities and family nights.

B lending families takes tremendous energy and work. It is also a highly stressful situation. Some of that stress is relieved over time, as relationships deepen and trust develops. Some of it can also be relieved by fun and laughter, and by not taking everything so seriously.

Fun and laughter should be an integral part of stepfamily growth. It won't happen by itself though. Couples who work at having fun are more likely to find it, than those who wait for spontaneous outbursts of joyful family times.

Anxiety and tension are day-to-day realities for most people in our modern culture. But they are even more true for blended families.

Laughter can be a catalyst for change. It can bring people together. It can ease the pain in admitting our mistakes.

Unless blended families make moments of respite and create a place where laughter and fun can erupt, they may slide into discouragement or despair.

This session does not make light of the vital and serious task stepparents face in integrating their family. Instead, it calls them to look for and create bright spots along the way.

Couples who work at having fun are more likely to find it.

Getting Ready

Scripture:
Proverbs 15:15; 17:22;
I Peter 1:8.

1. Prepare copies of "Family Fun Idea Sheet (RS-12A) and "Ideas for Family Activities" (RS-12B). Be sure to three-hole punch if necessary.
2. Read through "Watching Under the Stars" several times so you read it comfortably, and with inflection. If you have an opportunity, ask someone to listen to you read it before the session.
3. For Step 2, write the ideas for "How NOT to Have Fun" (see page 84) on the board or sheet of newsprint in advance. Keep covered until time to refer to it.
4. Have these items on hand: newsprint or board, Bibles, extra paper, pens.

❶ Looking for Light

Objective:
To help participants focus on finding slivers of laughter, fun, and togetherness in their family lives (10-15 minutes).

The following story was written by the author of these sessions. She is a remarried woman in a stepfamily.

Watching Under the Stars

What a year it was for our stepfamily. The children no longer children, facing the dangers and joys of adult life.

The youngest, at 17, had been in a car accident, barely escaping with her life. The oldest, Shelly, fell in love and married.

After the accident and before a late-summer wedding came a night of shooting stars. We had heard for days that this once-in-a-lifetime event was coming. A night, when, if we were lucky, the sky might blaze with lights, streaking and dancing for us.

That night Shelly called from her boyfriend's parents' house to remind us, "Don't forget to go outside after midnight and look up."

I wasn't so sure about the idea. I watched Andrea haul out binoculars and thought: Why should we subject ourselves to Michigan mosquitoes, damp night air, and sleeplessness? Compared to the remote chance of seeing a few shooting stars, my soft, warm bed sounded appealing.

But after the phone call, and seeing Andrea dig out dusty sleeping bags, I couldn't refuse. "Don't

Andrea was right. When you see a star, you know it.

expect too much, honey," I explained to the girl who had been walking again for only a few months. "They said the best sightings will be on the east coast."

The screen door in the rear of the house banged. David, my husband, Andrea's stepfather, ducked outside. I glanced at a clock—11:45. We followed with sleeping bags, binoculars, and pillows.

David called to us across the yard, "I don't see anything."

"They said you might not be able to see it with the naked eye," Andrea reminded us.

Then why bother, I thought irritably.

I don't know how long the three of us stood there, looking up, not even certain what to look for.

Into the dark silence, Andrea suddenly spoke, "I saw one."

David glanced at me and shrugged.

I said, "It was probably an airplane, Andrea."

She kept looking up. "I know a star when I see one, Mother."

I don't know why, but I turned my gaze to the corner of the sky she was watching. Within seconds, something streaked brightly across the black canvas, so quickly it hardly seemed real. But I knew better. I had seen it. It left glowing dots in my eyes. Andrea was right. When you see a star, you know it.

"There's another one, " I said, pointing.

"I didn't see anything," David said. "There's nothing there."

David is the most logical member of our blended family. If he can't see it, it doesn't really exist.

We kept gazing up and stepping backwards. Eventually, the three of us were out from under trees, on the golf course behind our house, watching a sky that seemed to roll on forever.

I was the first to unroll a sleeping bag and plop down. Then Andrea and finally David. The three of us lay very still, staring upward. We discovered that only by watching one small area intently could we see shooting stars. We had to resist the urge to let our eyes wander across the sky.

If we refuse to break our routine, to stop and be still, we might miss . . . a moment when light breaks in. . . ."

Before long, the logical one started counting. He stopped his count when it passed fifteen, not including what Andrea and I saw.

I won't forget the feel of that night or the silence and the sights. Into the darkness, one of us would call the others to watch: "I see one." "Look there it goes" "Over here."

Even though Shelly was away. I knew that she and her soon-to-be-husband were under the stars too, watching for streaks of beauty and experiencing that magical moment with us.

We stayed there until sleep began overtaking us. I wanted to hold the moment for our family, hold it forever. To catch and cherish the lights called from the sky. To look hard, keep still, and be together.

By the next morning, the stars were gone. We had wedding plans to finish and an appointment with a specialist for Andrea.

But it all seemed a little easier. I'd been reminded that it's possible to seek and find bright spots. Even in the grip of change and pain, we can have snatches of wonder, if we take time to linger.

For David and me, that night has been added to other magical moments we have shared in our stepfamily. The shooting stars will stay with us all our lives, along with choir concerts, the opening night of a play, our first vacation together, proms, graduation, softball games, marathon checker games, dancing in the kitchen.

It's so easy to live in the ordinary—to turn off the light and go to bed—rather than stay up watching the sky. But if we refuse to break our routine, to stop and be still, we might miss a moment that will never come again. A moment when light breaks in and we can point each other toward it and hold our breaths for the holiness of it all.[1]

After you have read the story. Ask: **What do you think the author wanted you to get from the story?**

There are no right and wrong answers in this discussion. The purpose is for participants to acknowledge the importance of carving out family time for fun and relaxation. (You can help the group discover this point by rereading the line, "If we refuse to break our routine, to stop and be still, we might miss a moment that will never come again. A moment when light breaks in. . . .")

We can help create moments of light for our families. These will help get us through the struggles that come with blending families. But, they won't just happen. We will have to be aware and we will have to work at it.

If you are working with the longer session, ask: **What "slivers of light" have you experienced in the midst of the challenges of blending families?**

Allow time for two or three people to share.

❷ For Your Family

Objective:
To help couples consider the interests of their families so they can better select activities for them (10-15 minutes).

When we go to the effort of planning, we want to be sure our families have fun. We don't want the event to turn into a complaint session with no one cooperating.

If it does flop, perhaps we've been following one of these rules for not having fun.

Write these on newsprint or the board in advance. Be sure to keep them out of sight until this part of the session. After reading each one, give the group a chance to think of an example they have seen of this. If they don't come up with any, use the one after each statement.

How NOT to Have Fun[2]

Be very assertive about having fun. (A mother who loved her life in the country forces her family to go on weekend hikes. "It will be good for you.")

Ignore the wishes and schedules of the children. (Especially true of junior high and high school students who feel more need for their peers than they do for you.)

Work so hard to schedule fun that you don't have fun. (Make such a detailed plan for fun that it becomes work.)

Be passive and uncertain about what to do. (Don't plan ahead. Instead, the whole family will sit around moping and disgusted because no one can think of anything to do.)

Act critical about an event or activity. (When the family decides they'd rather not take your idea, or something just isn't your favorite, you can ruin it for everyone with the wrong attitude.)

L *aughter relieves guilt, improves circulation, breaks tension, and helps give a new perspective.*

Ask a child or teenager to come up with an activity.
(Ask, "What do you want to do?" and then be frustrated because they just shrug. A better idea is to give them choices: "Do you want to go swimming or would you rather go to the zoo?")

Ask: **In what other ways do you think you can sabotage family fun?** Then pass out "Family Fun Idea Sheet" (RS-12A). Group members can do this alone or with their spouses. Give them time to work on it. Stress that every family is different.

The secret to successful family nights and activities is understanding what appeals to your own family and planning for what the whole family will enjoy.

❸ Laughter Cures and Heals

Objective:
To look at Scriptures about the benefits of laughter and a cheerful heart (5 minutes).

Ask volunteers to read aloud the following Scripture passages. After each one, ask the group what it tells us about laughter and good times.

Proverbs 15:15 (A cheerful heart can create "a continual feast" even in the midst of hard times.)
Proverbs 17:22 (A cheerful heart is good medicine for the spirit, bringing healing.)
I Peter 1:8 (A relationship with Christ fills us with joy which helps us cope with all circumstances.)

❹ Getting Down the Details

Objective:
To present specific ideas for family fun and have the couples choose their favorites (10 minutes).

Distribute copies of "Ideas for Family Activities" (RS-12B). Have the group members read through this list of activities that other families have tried. Instruct them to circle those that sound like good possibilities for their families and to put a star beside the ones they will develop a specific plan for in the next three months.

*L*aughter enhances hopefulness about what God is doing in our lives.

❺ Having Fun with Fun

Objective:
To have parents focus on additional benefits of laughter (10-15 minutes).

Divide the participants into two or three groups. Tell them to take notes on the following information.

According to experts, there are many benefits to laughter. These fall into five categories: emotional, physical, social, intellectual and spiritual.

EMOTIONAL—relieves guilt over minor blunders; eases fear and negative attitudes; brain releases natural antidepressants; eases adjustment to change; helps us accept our limits.

PHYSICAL—improves circulation and deepens breathing, causes release of natural painkillers (endorphins); helps digestion; improves sleep; lowers blood pressure; increases metabolic rate; improves immune system; lessens inflammation.

SOCIAL—breaks tension in strained relationships; provides an icebreaker; promotes vulnerability and honesty; generates a positive attitude.

INTELLECTUAL—allows clear thinking; helps give a new perspective to problem solving; aids creativity; breaks negative thought patterns.

SPIRITUAL—provides a blow to false pride; builds faith by improving an optimistic attitude; dispels a martyr complex; demonstrates the absurdity of perfectionism; enhances hopefulness about what God is doing in our lives.

When you are finished, tell the small groups to write a 15-second commercial for a new product: LAUGHTER. They can include music, dramatizations, whatever they'd like. Explain that each group will put on a commercial. Allow about five to ten minutes for groups to create their commercials.

At the end of the session, allow each group to put on their commercial. Keep the atmosphere light and fun. This is a good time for the group to relax and enjoy one another.

Close the session by praying that God will bring laughter and fun into the lives of our families and express thankfulness for the healing gift of laughter.

Notes:

1. Lonni Collins Pratt, "Watching Under the Stars," *Christian Living Magazine*, Nov. 1993, p. 8. Used by permission of the author.

2. Dr. Milton Schwebel, "How to Have Fun as a Family . . . and Learn Too," *Bottom Line*, July 30, 1991, p. 12.

Family Traditions All Your Own

13

Session Aim:
To help blended families establish new family traditions while affirming the old and growing toward unity.

Some people think of traditions as dusty, lifeless, and without merit. The meaning of tradition is simple. It is the passing on of knowledge, practices, and customs from one generation to the next. Even those who claim to be against traditions are influenced by them.

Traditions encompass some reality of our lives and mark that reality in time as important and not to be forgotten. Traditions are developed by repeating rituals that help us remember the important event. As we pass on the tradition, we also continue to relive the initial event.

The church has traditions such as communion and baptism that mark the radical new order of Christianity. These bring the essentials of our faith to remembrance. In the same way, family traditions keep alive and pass on to the next generation some core reality about a family.

Traditions also unite people and give them a sense of belonging and of being connected to those who have gone on before them and those who will come after them. It is one way to help give blended families a sense of longevity and stability.

As group members end their study, this session on tradition will remind them that they are not alone. There is hope for their families and they have an active part in successful family integration.

*T*raditions are the passing on of knowledge, customs, history, and practices to the next generation.

Getting Ready

Scripture:
Exodus 13:14, 17; Deuteronomy 6:4-9; 8:2; 8:10, 11; I Chronicles 16:11-13; I Corinthians 11:23-26; Psalm 77:11; Jeremiah 6:16.

1. Gather a collection of holiday items representing several different holidays, such as a cross for Good Friday, a star or angel for Christmas, a pilgrim for Thanksgiving, a flag for Independence Day, etc. Try to include these holidays: Christmas, Valentine's Day, Easter, New Year's Day, Palm Sunday, Thanksgiving, Independence Day, Good Friday, Mother's Day, Father's Day. It's fine to include more than one symbol of any holiday as long as you have a variety. Display these on a table in the room where the group meets. Be sure to look over Step 1 so you understand what you'll be doing with these items.
2. Prepare copies of "Tradition Drill" (RS-13A), "Passages for Remembering" (RS-13B), "Never Forget" (RS-13C), and "Traditions, Traditions!" RS-13D. Be sure to three-hole punch, if necessary.
3. You will need newsprint or board to write on, extra paper, Bibles, pens or pencils.

❶ Reflecting on Tradition

Objective:
To help group members recognize the value and meaning of traditions (10 minutes).

As group members arrive, have paper and pencils available and ask each person to take one of the decorations or symbols off the table. Begin the session with the following comments:

All of us are consciously or unconsciously developing and living out certain traditions. Traditions are the passing on of knowledge, customs, history, and practices to the next generation. The most obvious incidence of this involves holidays.

Each participant has a symbol of a holiday. Ask each one to think about the traditions around that holiday and to write briefly about his or her enjoyment of those traditions. Allow a few minutes for writing.

Ask for three volunteers to talk about the traditions and memories connected with their symbols. When they have finished, ask the group to describe how tradition has influenced the volunteers.

Acknowledge that to some people, traditions have a negative connotation, especially with the Baby Boom generation. Chances are, your group includes many Baby Boomers. Take time to dispel negative images of traditions by stressing that the important quality of tradition is the remembering.

If time permits, read this quote from Frederick Buechner: **"Remembering gives us stability. It reminds us of** what we know to be true by experience.

"How they do live on, those giants of our childhood, and how well they manage to take even death in their stride . . . it can never put an end to our relationships with them. Wherever or however else they may have come to life since, it is beyond a doubt that they live still in us. Memory is more than looking back to a time that is no longer; it is looking out into another kind of time altogether where everything that ever was continues not just to be, but to grow and change with the life that is. The people we loved. The people who loved us. The people who, for good or ill, taught us things."[1]

Write this definition of *tradition* on the board, and encourage participants to copy it in their notes:

Tradition is the transmission of knowledge, practice, custom, and history from generation to generation.

When you have finished, underline each word and say: **This is what tradition does. It underlines the important. It reminds our children to remember. It says, "Pay attention, this is important."** The challenge for parents is to create significant traditions rather than meaningless ones. This is crucial to blended families because they come together without a joint history. Traditions that integrate the past, present, and future can be part of stepfamily integration.

❷ The Godly Tradition

Objective:
To help participants learn how God used tradition to form a covenant community (10-15 minutes).

Pass out "Tradition Drill" (RS-13A). Tell group members they have fifteen seconds to associate a festival or tradition with its symbol.

Answer key—(Thanksgiving–cornucopia; Passover–lamb; Christians–ichthus or fish; communion–cup and grapes; the flood–ark; Ten Commnadments–two tablets; Hanukkah–menorah or candlestick; marriage–bride and groom hands with ring; graduation–graduation caps; Jesus Christ–three crosses; Easter–soldier by tomb; post-flood covenant–rainbow; Christmas–Mary, Joseph, and baby Jesus)

Most of the group will finish easily. Those who don't will still make easy and strong connections between the symbol and the reality.

When they have finished, ask this question:
What is the benefit of connecting a reality to a sym-

God used tradition to underline the things He did not want forgotten.

bol? (It is easy to remember. You connect it to the symbol without even thinking about it. The symbol wraps up a multitude of imagery into one simple form.)

Pass out "Passages for Remembering" (RS-13B). Have participants do this Bible study in couples. (If you have married persons attending without their spouses, pair them up together or with yourself.) After reading the passage together, tell them to write down key words and phrases which relate to traditions and remembering.

Discuss their discoveries when they have finished, suggesting the following as key words, if they are not mentioned by group members.

Exodus 12:14, 17—(commemorate, celebrate, festival to the
   Lord, lasting ordinance, generations to come)
Deuteronomy 6:4-9; 8:2; 8:10, 11—(upon your hearts, impress
   them on your children, talk about them, tie them as symbols
   on your hands, bind them on your foreheads, write them,
   remember, in order to know, do not forget, failing to ob-
   serve)
I Chronicles 16:11, 12—(look, see, remember)
I Corinthians 11:23-26—(I received, I passed, remembrance of
   me, proclaim the Lord's death)
Psalm 77:11—(I will remember)

For further discussion, use these questions:
**How extensively has God used traditions in the cov-
enant family?** (We see it throughout both Old and New Testa-
ments.)

What is the purpose of these traditions? (To cause us to remember and proclaim God's faithfulness. God used tradition to underline the things He did not want forgotten. This is exactly what parents in blended families can do.

Traditions are a way of remembering, but also a way of finding direction. The people of Abraham clung to the stories of their parents because they heard God speaking in them and through those events, speaking not only in the past, but also in the situations they faced. These were a history of God's faithfulness and also a history of the formation of the covenant people.)

Have a volunteer read Jeremiah 6:16.
**What is the promise mentioned in this passage for
following the traditional paths set out by the Lord?** ("You
will find rest for your souls.")

Tradition just for the sake of tradition is meaningless.

❸ Teaching the Children to Remember

Objective:
To give suggestions for establishing traditions in blended families (15-20 minutes).

We mentioned earlier in the session that tradition just for the sake of tradition is meaningless. In each instance when God established a tradition, He was underlining something important to remember.

We should keep this in mind when we establish traditions for our family.

Distribute "Never Forget" (RS-13C). Give group members a few minutes to look it over. Suggest that they spend some time praying about what is most important for their children to remember and take time to identify the things most important to pass on.

After participants have had time to work on this sheet, set it aside for a moment and ask participants to brainstorm a list of holidays and events around which traditions can be built. Jot their ideas on the board or sheet of newsprint. The group's list may look something like this:

(Family anniversaries
Holidays
Birthdays
Mealtimes
First time events: first day of school, first after-school job, learning to ride a bike, driver's license, etc.
Routine events: visitation, going to school, weekends, etc.
Beginnings and endings
Losses
Celebrations
Vacations
Seasons, etc.)

Encourage participants to copy these "tradition possibilities" for future reference. Ask them to consider: **What kinds of events and activities could be developed around these "tradition possibilities" which would help you pass on the important things you circled on the "Never Forget" resource sheet (RS-13C)?**

Discuss possibilities as a group. (For example, when a child celebrates a birthday, give him or her a rolled-up "diploma" tied with a ribbon which outlines new *responsibilities and privileges* that go along with the child's new age. This would help the whole family remember that the child is growing up, reinforce that this child has special gifts, and a special place in the family.) Suggest they keep this list of "tradition possibilities" with the previous resource sheet to use when developing plans.

When several people have suggested possibilities, pass out resource "Traditions, Traditions!" RS-13D for their consideration at home.

❹ Wrapping It All Up

Objective:
To give participants a chance to discuss the sessions they have participated in and recognize their growth (10-15 minutes).

For thirteen weeks group members have been together exploring the many complications, challenges, and joys of being part of a stepfamily. Take these last few minutes together to talk about what they have learned and how they have grown. Challenge them to think about this question:

What have you learned in the last thirteen weeks and what are you going to do to strengthen your blended family?

Leave ample time for prayer and good-byes. If time allows, encourage sharing from different participants. Close the session by praying for each family by name and asking God to bring them together and give them a daily sense of His presence and love.

Notes:

1. Frederick Buechner, *The Sacred Journey* (New York: Harper San Francisco, 1982), p. 21.

Bibliography

Augsburger, David. *Caring Enough to Forgive.* Ventura, Calif.: Regal Books, 1981.

_____. *Sustaining Love, Healing & Growth in the Passages of Marriage.* Ventura, Calif.: Regal Books, 1988.

Bilezikian, Gilbert. *Beyond Sex Roles.* Grand Rapids, Mich.: Baker, 1985.

Bloomfield, Harold H. *Making Peace in Your Stepfamily.* New York: Hyperion, 1993.

Clapp, Rodney. *Families at the Crossroads.* Downers Grove, Ill.: InterVarsity Press, 1993.

Coleman, William. *What You Should Know About Getting Along With a New Parent.* Minneapolis: Augsburg, 1992.

Davidson, Jeff. *Breathing Space.* New York: Master Media, 1991.

Duty, Guy. *Divorce and Remarriage.* Minneapolis, Minn.: Bethany Fellowship, 1967.

Einstein, Elizabeth. *Strengthening Your Stepfamily.* Circle Pines, Minn.: American Guidance Service, 1986.

Erwin, Gayle. *The Jesus Style.* Waco, Tex.: Word Books, 1988.

Foster, Richard J. *Celebration of Discipline.* San Francisco: Harper & Row, 1978).

Glassman, Bruce. *Everything You Need to Know about Stepfamilies.* New York: Rosen Publishing Group, 1993.

Johnston, Jon. *Walls or Bridges: How to Build Relationships that Glorify God.* Grand Rapids, Mich.: Baker, 1988.

Joy, Donald. *Rebonding: Preventing and Restoring Damaged Relationships.* Waco, Tex.: Word Books, 1986.

Keener, Craig. *And Marries Another.* Peabody, Mass.: Hendrickson Publishers, 1991.

Richards, Larry. *Remarriage: A Healing Gift from God.* Waco, Tex.: Word Books, 1981.

Sande, Ken. *The Peacemaker.* Grand Rapids, Mich.: Baker, 1991.

Visher, Emily B. and Visher, John S. *Old Loyalties, New Ties: Therapeutic Strategies with Stepfamilies.* New York: Brunner/Mazel Inc., 1988.

Wangerin, Walter, Jr. *As for Me and My House.* Nashville, Tenn.: Thomas Nelson, 1990.

Weber, Stu. *Tender Warrior.* Three Sisters, Ore.: Multnomah Books, 1993.

Wilke, Steve and Dave and Neta Jackson. *When It's Hard to Trust.* Wheaton, Ill.: Tyndale House Publishers, 1991.

_____. *When We Can't Talk Anymore.* Wheaton, Ill.: Tyndale House Publishers, 1991.

Wright, H. Norman. *The Power of a Parent's Words.* Ventura, Calif.: Regal Books, 1991.

Wright, Linda Raney. *A Cord of Three Strands.* Old Tappan, New Jersey: Fleming H. Revell, 1987.

A Portrait of Our Family

Draw a simple line or stick-figure portrait of each family member with age and name. Also write down one thing that person enjoys.

How many people live in your household?

How many family members live in a different household?

What experience as a stepfamily has brought you the most joy?

Each of you list one expectation you have of your stepfamily.

Wife:

Husband:

Great Expectations

You were asked to respond quickly on a separate sheet of paper to help you answer most honestly. To the left of each statement, record your initial response. You will use the blank following each statement at the end of this session.

___ 1. I expect my spouse to ease the burden I've carried as a single parent. _____

___ 2. I expect my spouse to make me happy. _____

___ 3. I expect myself to feel positive and loving toward my stepchildren. _____

___ 4. I expect my stepchildren to love me. _____

___ 5. I expect to exercise parental authority over my stepchildren. _____

___ 6. I expect conflict in our stepfamily. _____

___ 7. I expect to handle our problems without outside help. _____

___ 8. I expect our children to get along. _____

___ 9. I expect my spouse to love my children. _____

___10. I expect my children to respect my spouse. _____

___11. I expect my spouse to respect my children. _____

___12. I expect a full partnership in making family decisions. _____

___13. I expect my spouse to be the leader in our household. _____

___14. I expect my life to be better now that I'm married. _____

___15. I expect to help my stepchildren solve their problems. _____

Expectation Adjustments

Briefly review your responses on RS-1B, then read the following:

1. I am not a victim, and others don't owe me anything.
2. No other person is responsible to make me happy.
3. I am not responsible to make others happy either.
4. Others are not villains, they are sufferers who hurt others when they are hurt.
5. God alone can meet human expectations of perfect love, abiding presence, and unquestioning acceptance.

Refer back to the "Great Expectations" resource sheet (RS-1B). To the right of each "Great Expectation" on RS-1B record the number of one of the above attitudes which might change your earlier response. Draw on the discoveries you gathered from the Bible study portion of the session. (For example, if you answered in agreement with number fourteen, you might now want to jot number 5 next to it from the above list.) Not all expectations on RS-1B are problematic if they are handled with care. These "expectation adjustments" merely bring a new perspective.

When you have finished, use the space below to rewrite the five principles at the top in your own words, applying them to your specific life situation. Feel free to share these rewritten principles with your spouse.

1.

2.

3.

4.

5.

Who Really Matters?

The datebook below represents a twenty-four hour period which is the amount of time each of us has every day to serve God and love our spouse. In the spaces provided, summarize what you are usually doing or thinking about at that time. Use last Sunday, or another recent Sunday, as an example. Be as detailed as possible.

Sunday

6 A.M. _____

7 A.M. _____

8 A.M. _____

9 A.M. _____

10 A.M. _____

11 A.M. _____

12 A.M. _____

1 P.M. _____

2 P.M. _____

3 P.M. _____

4 P.M. _____

5 P.M. _____

6 P.M. _____

7 P.M. _____

8 P.M. _____

9 P.M. _____

10 P.M. _____

11 P.M. _____

12 P.M. _____

1 A.M. _____

2 A.M. _____

3 A.M. _____

4 A.M. _____

5 A.M. _____

Pictures of a Marriage

On the easel below each title, draw a picture that reflects each phrase. Do not use words.

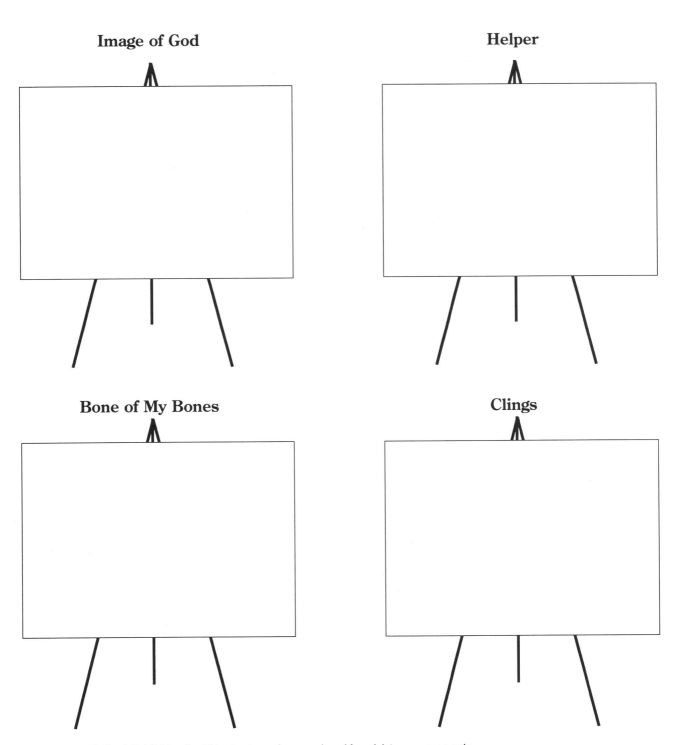

Image of God

Helper

Bone of My Bones

Clings

Intimacy Busters

Here are some ways people avoid intimacy. After discussing each and thinking of examples that demonstrate the behavior, your small group should pick one from the list and show the other groups how this behavior hinders intimacy. You may simply explain, perform a short skit, or write a poem.

- Shrug it off, act like you don't care.

- Make a joke or laugh.

- Change the subject.

- Act stronger than you feel.

- Become clinical and analytical.

- Withdraw into silence.

- Intimidate with anger.

- Act wounded or confused by it all.

- Talk to cover feelings.

- Suddenly find something urgent to do.

- Remove self physically or emotionally.

- Try to make spouse feel guilty.

- Become defensive.

Actions Speak Louder Than Words

1. *Make a date every week to do something together. Pick out times and mark your calendars. Take turns making the plans.*

2. *Find an activity to enjoy together. This needs to be mutually enjoyable—not he goes fishing and she tags along or she likes to ski and he throws logs on the fire.*

3. *Develop a list of "ours": our books, our favorite restaurant, our favorite CD, our sport, our photo album, our quilt, our recipe for spiced tea, etc.*

4. *Whenever possible, have serious discussions with the children, together. While this won't always work, make it your goal. It helps remind the children that you are a united front.*

5. *Set time every day to be alone and talk, even if it is only for a cup of coffee in the morning.*

6. *Create a spot in the house that is "yours." For example, a love seat next to a reading light or stereo for reading good books, quiet times, and intimate discussion.*

7. *Keep a scrapbook that records the history of your courtship and marriage. This should be a joint project.*

8. *Read a book about marriage—together.*

Ghosts from Yesterday

Note: Each of these incidents happened in the life of a real couple in their second marriage.

1. As a treat, she brings him fresh cherries to the office, plopping the bowl on his desk while he talks on the phone. He's been having a difficult time explaining a complicated situation to a customer. When he glances up at his wife, terror seems to strike her across the face and she begins whispering, "I'm so sorry . . ." over and over.

2. He stops to see his wife at the hospital where she's a nurse. It's her "lunch hour," but she works nights, so it's quite late. He finds her in the cafeteria munching chips and laughing with a handsome male co-worker. He leaves without her knowing he was there.

3. He's outside changing the tire on her car. It's snowing. The wind is blowing, and he will be late for work. "I'd better stay away until he's calmed down," she thinks.

4. She goes to bed with a sinus infection and sore throat. He feels romantic. She hates disappointing him, so she cooperates when he initiates lovemaking. After she falls asleep, he wonders if any women enjoy sex.

Journal Starters

Complete the following statements as part of your personal devotions over the next few weeks.

I feel loved when . . .

We are getting better at . . .

I am blessed because . . .

I recognize the gift of remarriage when . . .

I know I'm making progress when . . .

The most hopeful thing about our future is . . .

I like it when . . .

I feel I have failed because . . .

I feel disloyal when . . .

I miss . . .

I resent it when . . .

It hurts when . . .

I'm nervous about . . .

I feel scared that . . .

I feel trapped when . . .

I can be brave if . . .

Stepping into the Future

According to David Augsburger in *Caring Enough to Forgive*, the following is a summary of the steps that lead to forgiveness. You may have to take these steps many times before you begin to feel unthreatened or unafraid of more hurt.

> Step 1. Recognize the worth of the offender, regardless of the wrong done.
>
> Step 2. Cancel demands on the past by admitting it is unchangeable.
>
> Step 3. Work through anger to the point of trusting others and risking again.
>
> Step 4. Drop demands for ironclad guarantees of no more pain or misbehavior; this opens the promise of the future.
>
> Step 5. Connect with others, feel genuine love and forgiveness; opens the potential of healthy relationships again.

You can apply each step to yourself or others. In the blank space below briefly describe a situation where you or someone else in your blended family has been hurt. Then review the above steps and paraphrase the next step to healing. Personalize your paraphrase by using the actual names.

Adapted from David Augsburger, *Caring Enough to Forgive* (Ventura, Calif.: Regal Books, 1981), pp. 70-76.

When You Need Help

RS-3D

Prayerfully read the list below, asking God to enable you to be honest. (Any one of these is an indication that professional counseling should be sought.)

1. Physically hurting ourselves or others
   a. violence and abuse
   b. emotional, spiritual abuse
   c. substance abuse
2. Severe, prolonged depression
3. Inability to feel our pain or react to it
4. Refusal to accept responsibility
5. Accepting total blame and condemnation
6. Behavior that is destructive to relationships
7. Loss of ability to function at school or work
8. Deterioration of peer relationships
9. Withdrawal emotionally or physically
10. Compulsive behavior
11. Panic attacks, unreasonable fears
12. Sense of reality lost
13. Manipulation of others
14. Loss of sexual interest or unusual obsession with sex

Enabling Communication

Go over these suggestions for building communication with your ex-spouse. Check those you would like to try.

☐ 1. Write an agenda for what must be discussed. Stick to it. Avoid digressing or becoming emotional.

☐ 2. In some situations it will be possible to work toward similar rules in both houses. Consider these: bedtimes, meals, curfews, television, homework, etc.

☐ 3. Talk with the ex, while your spouse is present if this is possible. The new spouse should be present for support, rather than active participation in the discussion.

☐ 4. Keep a calendar for your children with their other parent's schedule, including drop off and pick up times, events, work hours, etc.

☐ 5. Send the children's parent a schedule of the school year, including special events, vacations, half-days, days off, etc. When something special is happening, such as a concert or sporting event, remind the children to call and invite their parent.

☐ 6. For holidays and birthdays, make plans a year in advance whenever possible and write out the arrangements.

☐ 7. For birthdays, Christmas, Father's Day, Mother's Day, etc., take your child shopping for a gift for his or her other parent. Often, children will be reluctant to ask.

Problems and More Problems

Discuss the best way to resolve the following problems within the biblical guidelines of peace and wisdom.

Problem 1: Because Timmy stayed up late watching television while overnight at his mother's house, he didn't study for his test and fell asleep in math class Monday morning.

Problem 2: Your ex-husband has agreed to return the children to your house by 8 P.M. Christmas Eve. He calls at 10:30 P.M. and says his mother would like to keep the children overnight and she will bring them home in the morning.

Problem 3: Julie is seven years old and lives with her mom. Her mother insists she go to bed at 8 P.M. One night she responded with, "Daddy lets me stay up until 10."

Problem 4: Twelve-year-old Michael tells you his mother has a different man spending the weekend with them than she did last month. He asks, "Why can't I be alone with Mom?"

Problem 5: Laticia is disappointed when her father doesn't show up for a school play. You don't recall that anyone thought to call him about it.

Playing with Power

Within your small group roleplay your assigned scene. If you do not have a role, take notes to aid group discussion.

SCENE 1

Players: Stepfather, stepdaughter or stepson (fourteen years old).
Situation: The stepchild is watching television when the stepfather gets home from work and wants to watch the evening news. Here is how the scene starts:

Stepfather: Please change the station to the news.
Child: I'm watching this.
Stepfather: Well, go do your homework. I want to watch the news!

Continue as you think the scene would play out.

SCENE 2

Players: Stepmother, father, and child (ten years old).
Situation: The stepmother has finished washing linens and leaves a neatly folded pile on her stepchild's unmade bed. After dinner, she discovers the linens are still there and the bed unmade.

Stepmother (to child): Did you see the sheets on your bed?
Child: Yeah, I saw them. I'll make the bed before I go to sleep.
Stepmother: You've had plenty of time already.
Father (to child): Please make your bed now.
Child (to father): Mom always made it for me!

Continue as you think the scene would play out.

SCENE 3

Players: Wife, husband.
Situation: A couple is discussing plans for a holiday dinner. They are trying to coordinate the schedule of the wife's children (who live with the couple) and the husband's children (who live nearby with their mother).

Wife: You may tell your children we'll eat at 3 P.M.
Husband: I don't think that's a good time, they won't be finished eating at their mother's house yet.
Wife: But my kids' dad is picking them up at 4.
Husband: Unless it's really inconvenient to change your cooking schedule, I prefer that we eat later. You know my kids don't spend as much time here as yours do, so I have to insist.

Continue as you think the scene would play out.

Leadership Turned Upside Down

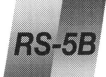

RS-5B

On the left under the reference, write the world's view as noted by the key words. On the right side, under the upside down reference, describe how what Jesus says about leadership is "upside down" compared to the world's view of leadership.

World's View	Key Words	Jesus' View
Genesis 1:27, 28		Ephesians 5:22-33 Genesis 1:27, 28
Mark 9:35		Mark 9:35
Matthew 18:3, 4		Matthew 18:3, 4
Matthew 20:25-28		Matthew 20:25-28

Your Own Style

RS-6A

While not strictly limited to these, here are five possible styles of conflict management. Next to each style, write names or draw sketches of extended family members you think fit this style. Put a star next to your own.

Avoiding Dislikes unpleasant situation and denies there is a problem or refuses to deal with it. Resistant.	
Accommodating Automatically gives in to keep the peace at any cost. This person becomes heavily burdened and internalizes stress.	
Compromising Meets others halfway on issues where there is no obvious guilt or fault. Understands there is not just one way to handle a problem.	
Competing Starts with assumption that there are only two possible outcomes to the situation—winning or losing. Aggressively pursues own interest for possibly vain and prideful reasons.	
Collaborating Considers teamwork as most productive way to work out conflict. Encourages group communication and behaves fairly with the best of the group in mind.	

Stepping toward Peace

On the right side of this sheet, list questions you could ask yourself or actions to take in response to the biblical principle. If assigned, do this exercise in a group.

Principle 1: **Glorify God** I Corinthians 10:31—11:1	
Principle 2: **Get the log out of my own eye** Matthew 7:3-5 Lamentations 3:40 Galatians 6:4, 5	
Principle 3: **Go and show your brother his fault** Galatians 6:1, 2 Matthew 18:15 Ephesians 4:15, 29	
Principle 4: **Go and be reconciled** Colossians 3:12-15 Luke 6:27-33	

Communication Checklist

☐ 1. I will listen without distraction, without formulating a response, and without interrupting.

☐ 2. I will remain physically and emotionally with you, even during conflict.

☐ 3. I won't control or manipulate with sarcasm, bribery, threats, guilt, or emotionalism.

☐ 4. I will not blame you for how I feel.

☐ 5. Nothing you say to me will ever be used against you.

☐ 6. I'll be as honest and vulnerable as I know how.

☐ 7. I will love you unconditionally as God loves us.

☐ 8. For the long haul, I'll work with you to break down the walls that divide us.

☐ 9. It is okay to disagree with me; I don't have to be right.

☐ 10. I will respect your need to tell me only what you can trust me with today and pray you will trust me more tomorrow.

☐ 11. I will respect you as the person God has created, gifted in ways I don't always understand. I will not speak or act in a demeaning manner.

☐ 12. I will work hard at not letting the sun go down on my anger. I will keep short accounts.

Working toward Resolution

This work sheet will help you write a plan for conflict resolution. Feel free to make copies for other members of your family.

Issue to be resolved:

Actions to take:

Who is responsible for each action:

Completion dates for action:

When and how results will be reviewed:

Question for self-reflection (Check the standard that best matches yours):
What yardstick am I using to judge a behavior or offense?

- ☐ What others will think

- ☐ How I was raised

- ☐ Cultural standards

- ☐ Unquestioned but always accepted biblical ideas

- ☐ Convictions and beliefs I have developed through personal growth, experience, Bible study, prayer, and meditation.

- ☐ Pride or hurt feelings

Stepparent Quiz Bowl

1. What percentage of stepchildren have no contact with their biological father?
   (75 percent.)

2. Who exhibits more behavior problems after a divorce, boys or girls?
   (Boys.)

3. Who exhibits more behavior problems after remarriage, boys or girls?
   (Girls.)

4. Who seems to have the most stressful role, stepfather living with stepchildren, or stepmother living with stepchildren?
   (Stepmother.)

5. What is the best predictor of stepmother unhappiness?
   (Having a stepdaughter. The stepmother/stepdaughter relationship is considered the most difficult. This is true whether or not the stepdaughter resides with her. Those women who have all female stepchildren top the "unhappiness" list.)

6. Children of what age seem to have the most problem adjusting to stepparents: preschool, elementary age, young teenagers, middle teenagers, or young adults?
   (Young teenagers [12-16] have the most difficulty.)

7. True or False: Stepfather families, those in which the man is the stepparent, have the least amount of stress.
   (True. Children especially experience the least amount of stress when living with their mother and stepfather.)

8. How many emotional stages can a stepfamily expect to go through to reach integration?
   (Either seven or eight, according to which researchers you consult. These stages will be explored more fully in Session 10 with resource sheet, "Stepfamily Stages" RS-10B.)

9. What is the main factor in determining how long stepfamily integration usually takes?
   (The age of the children. With children elementary age or younger, integration can happen as soon as 18 months or two years. With teenagers and young adults, it takes many more years.)

10. What is the most difficult area of adjustment for adolescents in stepfamilies?
    (Discipline.)

11. True or False: Young adults from blended families tend to leave home at a younger age than their peers.
    (True.)

12. True or False: The most successful stepparents are those who become actively involved right away in disciplining stepchildren.
    (False. Stepparents who quickly assume the role of disciplinarian seem to delay and hinder the process of family integration.)

13. True or False: Children who have limited contact with their noncustodial parent adjust better to a stepparent.
    (False. Just the opposite is true.)

Adapted from Emily B. Visher and John S. Visher, *Old Loyalties, New Ties: Therapeutic Strategies with Stepfamilies* (New York: Brunner/Mazel, Inc., 1988), pp. 44-61.

Weighing Your Shoulds

Read over this list of "dangerous shoulds" that sometimes motivate adults to discipline. Think about the difference between these "shoulds" as motivations for disciplining a child and what you learned from Scripture. At the bottom of the sheet, fill the box labelled "My shoulds" with those you recognize in yourself.

Absurd superhuman shoulds:
Good children should never talk back to their parents.
I should be able to make you behave.

Guilty shoulds:
When grandparents come over you should iron the sheets.
When the neighbors are outside, you should play quietly with your sister.

Yesterday shoulds:
The way our parents told us should be the way it's done.
My father mowed grass on Saturday; grass should be mowed on Saturday.

Shoulds we don't understand:
No one should sleep after 10 A.M.
I don't know why, that's just the way it is.

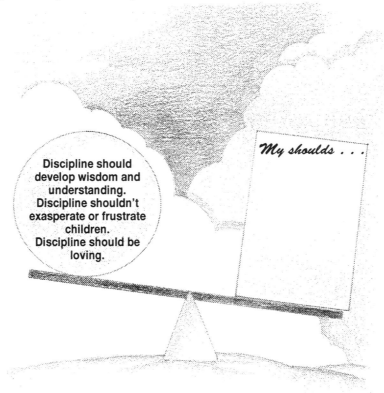

Discipline should develop wisdom and understanding.
Discipline shouldn't exasperate or frustrate children.
Discipline should be loving.

My shoulds . . .

Tips for Stepparents

1. Let children develop a relationship with you at their own pace and in their own style. You will never force them to accept you.

2. Enjoy each child and get to know him or her. Spend one-on-one time together (when the child is ready for it). You should be more adult friend and guide, less parental authority.

3. Express your willingness and enthusiasm for a relationship. However, make sure the child knows you aren't trying to replace his or her biological parent.

4. Don't try too hard. Be yourself. Accept the limits that exist in the relationship.

5. Be honest about your own apprehensions and uncertainty. This helps the child feel safe enough to talk too.

6. Create emotional safety by keeping promises and not judging the child as bad or wrong for how he or she feels.

7. Keep your heart open to the child's loss, be willing to grieve with them and share their pain. Acknowledge that it's okay to grieve.

8. Support your spouse when he or she disciplines, but don't make the mistake of becoming an "authority" figure too soon.

9. When instances occur where you must enforce limits with a step-child, rely on the established authority of your spouse. Say things such as, "Would your mother want you to watch that television show?" Or "Your father will be gone tonight. Before he left, he suggested you clean the garage."

10. Follow the child's lead in what to call you.

11. Love takes time to grow, so don't expect to feel loving. However, you can work to be fair and understanding from the beginning of the relationship.

The Cycle of Anger

Most conflicts with children occur as a result of discipline. When we react to what others are doing, we are easily caught in a cycle of anger.

In the cycle below, chart a disciplinary problem you are now struggling with. Beside each key phrase, identify what is happening (i.e., what you/child are doing, thinking, feeling as you each react to the actions/behavior of the other).

CHILD _____   ME _____

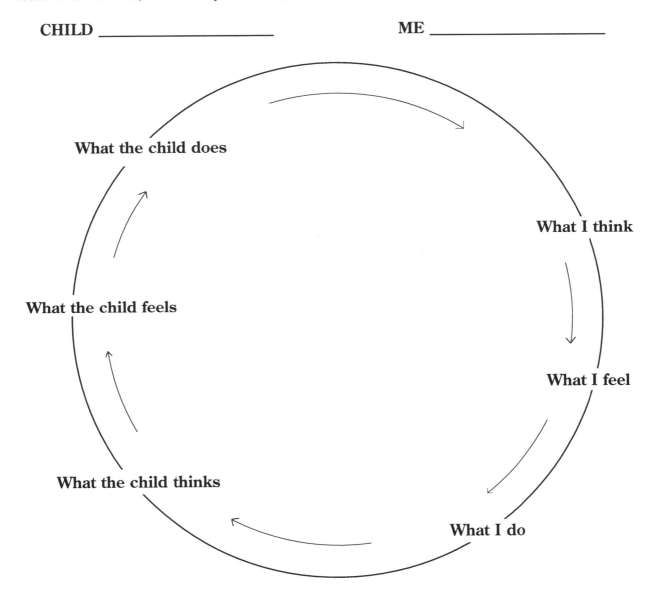

What the child does

What I think

What the child feels

What I feel

What the child thinks

What I do

Make photocopies of this sheet to help you chart other disciplinary problems with different children, or to help you understand what is happening when you have a conflict with this same child in the future.

The Tyranny of Choice

RS-8A

Use the following codes to indicate how often you make each of the decisions listed below:

M = *monthly (or less)*
W = *weekly*
D = *daily*
★ = *continually*

_____ 1. What brand of shampoo to use.

_____ 2. Which route to drive to work.

_____ 3. What movie to attend.

_____ 4. Which meal to pick off a menu.

_____ 5. Which greeting card to buy.

_____ 6. Where to go for an evening out.

_____ 7. What to watch on television.

_____ 8. What to make for dinner.

_____ 9. What task is most important to do today.

_____ 10. What book to buy.

_____ 11. Which devotional to use.

_____ 12. Which radio station to listen to.

_____ 13. What line to stand in.

_____ 14. When to eat lunch.

_____ 15. Which meeting or event to attend.

_____ 16. What chores must be done.

_____ 17. Who to call.

_____ 18. How to best finish a task quickly.

_____ 19. Where to sit.

_____ 20. Who to hold responsible.

_____ 21. Which toothpaste to buy.

_____ 22. Where to park your car.

_____ 23. How to do two things at once.

_____ 24. When or where to pray.

_____ 25. Which shoes to wear.

TALLY	
Monthly	_____
Weekly	_____
Daily	_____
Continually	_____
Total	**25**

Priority Pie

cleaning
cooking
eating
grooming
shopping
sleeping

exercise
solitude
devotions
education
hobby
worship

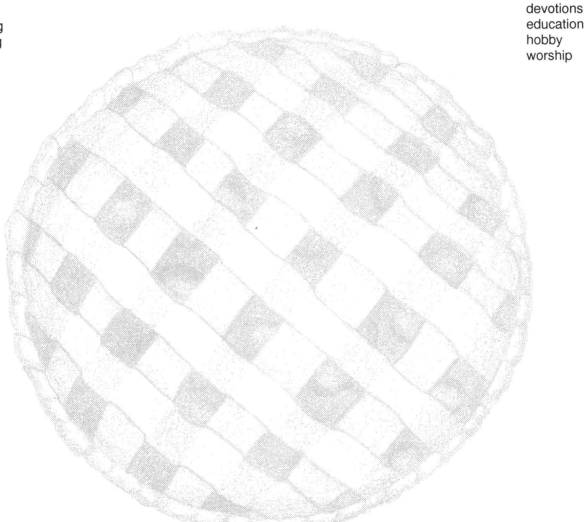

recreation
time with friends
couple time
time with each child
reading
family time

job
household repairs
serving others
children's activities
home/yard maintenance
family vacations

Stepfamily Tasks

These are the tasks stepfamilies usually accomplish on their way to integration. You may wish to keep these in mind when developing your own goals.

1. Dealing with losses and changes
Identify loss for all family members
Support expressions of grief
Help children talk and not act out
Read stepfamily books together
Make necessary changes slowly
See that everyone gets a turn
Accept insecurity of change
Keep children informed of plans concerning them

2. Negotiating different needs
Take a child development class
Learn more about different life stages
Communicate needs clearly
Negotiate incompatible needs
Develop tolerance and flexibility

3. Establishing new traditions
Recognize these are different, not right or wrong
Concentrate on what is important only
Stepparents take on discipline slowly
Have family meetings
Shift "givens" as little as possible
Retain and combine appropriate rituals
Create new traditions

4. Developing as a couple
Establish couple as primary, lifelong relationship
Nourish couple relationship
Plan time alone
Decide general household rules as a couple
Support each other with the children
Expect and accept complicated feelings in stepparenting
Decide on money matters together
Make decisions together
Develop spiritually as a couple

5. Creating a parenting support group
Deal directly with parents in other households
Keep children out of middle
Refrain from talking negatively about other parents
Accept limits, control only what is yours to control
Avoid power struggles between households
Respect former spouse's parenting rights

Contribute own uniqueness to children
Develop an effective way to communicate between households

6. Forming new family relationships
Learn about other's past histories
Make time for children and stepchildren
Make time for parent/child relationship
Parent gives time and space to stepparent/ stepchild
Do not expect instant love or pressure individuals
Be fair to stepchildren even when you don't feel loving
Follow children's lead in what to call stepparent
Do fun things together
Develop an individual family spirituality
Be yourself and get to know each other

7. Accepting shifts in household
Encourage children to enjoy their households
Give children time to adjust to changes
Don't ask children to be "messengers" or "spies"
Consider teenager's desire to change residences
Respect privacy of individuals and households
Set boundaries on own household only
Provide personal space for nonresidential children
Plan special times for your household
Communicate changes in your household with each other

8. Risking vulnerability despite little cultural support
Include stepparents in school, church, sports events
Give legal permission for stepparent to act when needed
Develop stepparent/stepchild relationship apart from couple time
Stepparent demonstrates interest in stepchild
Find supportive groups
Remember all relationships involve risk
Consider adoption if situation allows

Adapted from Emily B. Visher and John S. Visher, *Stepfamily Workshop Manual* (Lincoln, Neb.: 1986), Appendix C. Used by permission.

Evaluating Activities

Before agreeing to a new activity or event, evaluate it according to these guidelines. This system works for everything from serving on a board to ironing shirts.

1. Does it advance any of my stated goals and objectives for self and family?

2. Is it something I am uniquely gifted to do, or linked to what I understand my spiritual giftedness to be? Am I the best person to do it at this present time?

3. Do I have to alter my schedule to fit it in? Am I willing to give or change what must be changed?

4. Am I accepting for the right reasons or do I feel put on the spot? Am I taking on this activity out of false expectations (does the rug really have to be vacuumed again)?

5. What happens if I don't do it? Are there any negative effects of simply not doing this thing?

Here are some additional suggestions for time management:
- **Streamline:** If an activity does not support a goal, drop it.
- **Focus:** Eliminate distractions like television and phone during family time.
- **Organize:** Make (and follow) personal to-do lists regularly.
- **Simplify:** Make standardized lists of correct sizes, medications, favorite brands, etc.
- **Eliminate clutter:** If you haven't used it in a year or two, give or throw it away.
- **Communicate:** Develop and maintain a family calendar of all activities and appointments.
- **Increase efficiency:** Group errands together.
- **Relax:** Plan to kick back and have fun.
- **Say no:** Know your limits and allow yourself to decline without feeling guilty.

© 1995 David C. Cook Publishing Co. This sheet may be reproduced for ministry purposes only.

Extending the Borders of Family

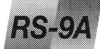

The Fatherhood of God beckons all people into a family relationship with one another. Blended families model this reality because some of our ties are biological and some are not.

Read the passages and answer the questions in each section.

• **All Christians are adopted into God's family; by rebirth we become "stepchildren."**
What benefits does this give us?

I John 3:1 _____

Romans 8:15-17 _____

John 1:12, 13 _____

II Corinthians 6:18 _____

• **Jesus Himself was part of a blended family. His human biological connection to Mary did not extend to Joseph. His siblings were half-brothers and half-sisters. Joseph's parents were His stepgrandparents. Jesus extended the borders of His family even farther. What was Jesus' definition of His "family"?**

Luke 2:48-52 _____

Luke 8:19-21 _____

What are some traits of these extended families we can model in our own blended families?

I John 3:13-15 _____

I John 3:16, 17 _____

I John 3:18 _____

Bridging the Gaps

Blended families face unique challenges because of their extensive family groups. Using the principles of love and self-sacrifice, discuss possible solutions for these situations faced by most blended families. Jot down helpful tips shared by others in the group.

1. **Holidays, birthdays, and other special events**
   Talk about what works for your family and how you have struggled.

2. **Staying in touch with a former spouse's family**
   What have you done to help your children retain a strong sense of connection to their roots?

3. **Family time**
   How do you guard time for your blended family to be together?

4. **Extended family relationships**
   In what specific ways can you encourage special relationships with extended family members such as cousins of similar ages or grandparents?

5. **New family ties**
   How can you develop ties with new steprelatives?

Record one thing that you can do immediately to help bridge the gaps in your new family.

A Place Where Trust Can Grow

Each of the following attitudes can prevent a trusting environment from developing in a home. In the space next to each numbered attitude, write an alternative (sometimes opposite) attitude that might foster more trust and acceptance.

1. My perspective is the right one.

2. Be logical.

3. Follow the rules.

4. Be practical.

5. Avoid ambiguity.

6. To err is wrong.

7. Play is a waste of time.

8. I don't do it that way.

9. Don't be foolish.

10. I'm not the creative sort.

Adapted from Roger von Oech, *A Whack on the Side of the Head* (New York, Warner Books, 1983), p. 9.

Stepfamily Stages

According to The Stepfamily Association of America, there are seven stages (some manuals break these into eight) stepfamilies can expect to pass through on the way to integration.

As honestly as possible, locate what stage your blended family is going through.

1. Fantasy
"We aren't going to have serious problems. Our situation is different."

2. Pseudo-Assimilation
"There's nothing to be worried about; of course we're fine." Underneath this is a growing sense that all is not well.

3. Awareness
"I know what's bothering me, but I can't talk about it yet." Person may be embarrassed or think his or her feelings are wrong.

4. Mobilization
"I don't like the way things are. You and I are going to have to do something." Dissatisfaction comes to surface, separation often happens here.

5. Action
"This is difficult, but somehow we'll work through it together." By shedding false expectations and fantasies, the couple begins working together.

6. Contact
"We're all getting closer. It will never be perfect." Stepfamily is able to handle day-to-day relationships and is developing genuine, deep relationships that will last.

7. Resolution
"Our family is different from others, but it's okay." Acceptance of what a blended family is and isn't. Problems still occur, but committed relationships provide a basis for working through differences.

Becoming a Bridge-Builder

Bridge Builders . . .

Extend selves to others

Focus on sharing and giving

See others as essential and needed

Encourage others

Lead to empowerment and unleashing

Wall Builders . . .

Protect selves

Focus on hoarding, possessing, accumulating

See others as a threat to security

Diminish others' usefulness

Lead to a sealed-off self

Adapted from Jon Johnston, *Walls or Bridges: How to Build Relationships that Glorify God* (Grand Rapids, Mich.: Baker, 1988), pp. 56-68.

The Spiritual Disciplines: A Primer

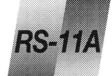

According to Celebration of Discipline, *the Christian classic by Richard Foster, the following are vital disciplines for spiritual formation. Use the space provided to jot down notes.*

Inward Disciplines	Outward Disciplines	Corporate Disciplines
Meditation	Simplicity	Confession
Prayer	Solitude (and silence)	Worship
Fasting	Submission	Guidance
Study	Service	Celebration

Adapted from Richard J. Foster, *Celebration of Discipline* (San Francisco: Harper and Row, 1978), pp. 3-10.

What do the following Scriptures tell me about spiritual disciplines?

II Corinthians 7:1	II Corinthians 10:3-5

For reflection:

• What disciplines are already part of my experience?

• In what disciplines do I need to grow?

• Which ones, if any, don't I understand?

Spiritual Development of Children

The following information on age-appropriate spiritual development is provided to help you understand your children better.

Preschool

Children are very self-centered and active. Books and devotions should focus on others, character-building, and simple concepts such as God loves you, be kind to others, be honest, there's nothing to be afraid of. Spend time reading to child.

Primary Age (5-7)

Children can understand more difficult concepts. They have concerns about death and being alone. They begin to read on their own, but still should be read to.

Intermediate (8-10)

Children are in an often confusing, stormy period. They dislike being preached to and prefer activity. Deal with topics relevant to the world they live in. Novels are good for this age; they like action and suspense.

Preteen (11-13)

These children are "tweeners." Some still have characteristics of the intermediate group and some are pushing hard toward the teen years. Girls are usually more sophisticated. They are seriously pondering their world and have questions about how God fits into it. Peers often become their measure of right and wrong, real and false.

Teens (14-17)

They are eager to think without being influenced by parents. They want independence. They often express indifferent feelings about God, church, and spirituality. Polls show they discuss spiritual matters among themselves. They will not tolerate prepackaged answers. They ask tough questions. Music is important to them. They have frequent sexual thoughts. Lively discussions and relevant topics are needed.

A Spiritual Plan

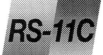

Here are some ideas for revitalizing your own spiritual life and developing family spirituality. After reviewing the suggestions and listing others, set and record your family goals in each time block. Write a few lines about what you hope your family spirituality will be like by then.

1. Get a book of prayers.
2. Begin building a library of resources.
3. Schedule a family prayer time.
4. Buy a Bible for each family member.
5. Schedule periods of silence.
6. Fast for one meal.
7. Select a family service project.

8. Family or individual retreat.
9. Begin a prayer list for family.
10. Develop holiday traditions.
11. Listen to Christian tapes, CDs.
12.
13.
14.
15.

One Week

One Month

Three Months

Six Months

One Year

Two Years

Three Years

Family Fun Idea Sheet

From this list, select:
1. *Circle the activities your child(ren) like to do.*
2. *Underline the things you personally enjoy. Place an "I" by ones you are interested in exploring.*
3. *Put a box around activities your spouse likes.*

Activity Ideas

zoo	crafts	roller skating
star-gazing	building	biking
swimming	gardening	local sightseeing
camping	hiking	photography
books	history	day trips
art	shopping	fairs and festivals
collecting something	farming	sporting events (soccer, football)
dramatics	mission work	
music	classic movies	carnival/theme park
craft classes	bowling	sailing/boating
archery	garage sales	air shows

Answer the following questions. Use the back or extra paper if you wish:

- **What activities did you enjoy most as a child?**

- **Recall something fun you did with one or both parents.**

- **Recall something fun you did with a sibling.**

- **How do you feel about your family when you remember these events?**

- **What time periods are available for family fun?**

- **What is unique about your state or region? (Lakes, mountains, historical sites, etc.)**

Ideas for Family Activities

Check activities you would like to try with your family. Put a star by any you will do within the next three months.

- Schedule a birthday art night including paints, chalk, and sketching for someone who likes art or is artistic. There are things you can get kids to do under the guise of, "Oh c'mon, it's your sister's birthday and this is important to her."

- Go to a public park for an afternoon. Play softball, ride the swings, have a picnic, fly a kite.

- In the spring, pick and label wildflowers. Bring a camera, too.

- Sleep under the stars on a warm night. Read with a flashlight, eat popcorn, try to figure out what constellations you're looking at with a book on astronomy.

- Plan a Meal of the Week. Everyone has to contribute something to it. You can also have theme meals. The theme can be ethnic, a color, or a type (for example, soup, salad, vegetable).

- Encourage stewardship of God's creation by driving in the country, tackling a cleanup project as a family, going to a nature preserve.

- Get a roadside geological guide and take a drive with it. Point out geological formations and differences. End with a picnic or dinner out.

- Make a family movie. Write the script, assign parts, shoot it together.

- Hold a family photo shoot at some remarkable site near your house. It could be in the mountains, near a lake, at a historical site. All family members have to be in the pictures.

- Have a family retreat. Plan it carefully to include quiet times, games, prayer, meals, exercise, reading, and rest. Don't allow electronic gadgets at all.

- Participate in a marathon or race as family. Have a sports night out that includes bowling, batting cage, miniature golf, and a swim at the local beach or public swimming pool.

- At dinner have everyone tell a story on the same theme: favorite birthday, first day of school, most embarrassing moment, what I like most about my best friend, etc.

- Go fishing.

- Visit a pick-it-yourself farm or pumpkin patch.

- Work on a project to enter in the local fair.

- Have a Kid's Night Out and take the kids to their favorite places.

- Hang an old white sheet on a wall and work on a family tree to put on display in the family room or den. (Make sure not to mark the wall through the sheet!)

- Play kickball by flashlight at night.

- Go rock hunting near lakes, streams, and rivers.

- Make a family calendar.

- Organize a church event together for blended families and single-parent families (combined): kite picnic, potluck, service project, ethnic dance night, etc.

- Have a no-electricity night. Be prepared with candles, books to read, puzzles, stories to tell, coloring books, or art projects.

- Have an "Honor Our Best Friends" night. Each person invites his or her best friend. Build pizzas together. Tell the story of your friendship. Watch a movie with a friendship theme.

- Keep an album of seasonal pictures. Try to capture your family mood for each season. Divide it by sections and include general autumn, winter, spring, and summer shots.

- Begin a family newsletter. Since blended family members don't all live in the same household, it can keep everyone informed. Twice a year is probably sufficient.

- With water-soluble paints, create a picture on a window facing the street. Change it with the seasons and happenings in the household.

Tradition Drill

Take 15 seconds to draw a line from the name of each tradition, event, or category to the appropriate symbol on the left or right.

Thanksgiving

Passover

Christians

Communion

The flood

Ten Commandments

Hanukkah

Marriage

Graduation

Jesus Christ

Easter

Post-flood Covenant

Christmas

Illustrations of tablets, soldier by tomb, cup and grapes, and lamb by Anne Kennedy.

Ark illustration taken from *52 Children's Programs for Church Time,* by Mary Rose Pearson, published by Accent Publications, Colorado Springs, Colorado. Copyright © 1986. Used with permission.

Passages for Remembering

After reading the Scriptures below, write down key words and phrases which relate to traditions and remembering.

Exodus 12:14, 17

Deuteronomy 6:4-9; 8:2, 10, 11

I Chronicles 16:11, 12

I Corinthians 11:23-26

Psalm 77:11

Never Forget

What do we want accomplished?
What do we want our children to learn?

There are many things you want your children to learn. On this work sheet, circle the ones in each category most important to you and add your own.

About God
Exclusivity of Jesus Christ
God loves you
God wants good for you
God will never leave you
God has been faithful
God can be trusted

_____

_____

_____

_____

About Living
Golden rule
Work hard
Take time to celebrate
Enjoy your life
Expect pain
God won't leave you

_____

_____

_____

_____

About Yourself
You need God
You are loved
You have gifts
You have a purpose
You are a sinner
You are a saint
You are special

_____

_____

_____

About Family
Family matters
Marriage is forever
Love unselfishly
Honor and respect
God's people are family
We love you and something of us will
   remain with you

_____

_____

_____

Traditions, Traditions!

• BEGIN A CALENDAR with Christian holy days and special events. Separate your traditions into steps and use the calendar to plan the work involved. Include children in the preparations.

• INCORPORATE EVERYDAY LIFE. You could give children a weekly blessing on Monday morning as a way to send them into the week. Read a psalm at every meal, or pray before the child goes to school. Traditions tell your children that you love them enough to develop special events even on ordinary days for their benefit.

• BUILD GOOD MEMORIES along with a sense of belonging to something that has been going on for a long time. Many children of divorce have reported feeling that their past is all a lie. This is a way to affirm their history while building a new family history.

• DRAW YOUR FAMILY TOGETHER. Incorporate inherited tradition with ethnic qualities. Create traditions for secular holidays also, such as Fourth of July, Memorial Day, Labor Day, etc. Include God in the celebration.

• AFFIRM INDIVIDUAL GIFTS AND PERSONALITIES. Consideration needs to be given to age, although often it is good for the sake of repetition that children begin early with a tradition and follow along until they come of age and understand the meaning behind the tradition.

• TALK ABOUT TRADITIONS TO-GETHER. Ask what is meaningful for the children and what they would like to continue. Incorporate old, familiar ones with new traditions whenever possible.

• ADJUST AS KIDS GROW. This is especially true as their understanding of certain events expand, such as Christmas and Easter.

• CAPTURE THE SPONTANEOUS. For example, one family lines up their snowy shoes on the porch on Christmas day as family members arrive. It is something a grandfather did years ago to make more sitting room and proudly display to the world that his family was home. Seventy-five years later it still speaks of love.

• BE ALERT TO WHAT IS MEANINGFUL. One mother who had always read "Cinderella" to her little girl gave her a copy of the book on her eighteenth birthday with an inscription that said, "I won't always be here to tuck you in and hear your prayers anymore. When you wish I could be, just read this book and remember."

• RECOGNIZE THE NEW, STRENGTHEN THE OLD. Parents should occasionally have a night out alone with each of their children. Stepparents can do the same when the child is ready for it. Siblings should have special times set apart for them. Often these kinds of events become traditions by eating at the same place, always going to a funny movie, listening to the same music, etc. Couples also must have special traditions that belong to them alone.

• THINK SEASONAL. Decorating the tree and yard or baking cookies at Christmas. Cider mills, pumpkin patches, and fall colors in autumn. Planting flowers and washing windows in spring. Whatever you do, keep in mind that your children will want to duplicate it with their own families, in another place and time. We can count on the seasons not to change.

• ASSOCIATE THINGS, TIME, AND LOCATION. Friday night for pizza, washing towels on Saturday morning, celebrating birthdays at a certain time of the day, coloring Easter eggs together, going to the same site for your weekend getaways time after time.

• RECORD YOUR TRADITIONS in a scrapbook with all the important details. Include a few pictures if you can. Also, if there are special items used in traditions, such as a certain recipe or special punch glasses, be sure these are set aside for the children to keep.